Happy 7

Simon

Regards   Mike Stimpson

The Cricket Professionals
of Oxford

Michael Stimpson

ACS PUBLICATIONS

First published in Great Britain by
Association of Cricket Statisticians and Historians
Bedford MK40 4FG.
© Michael Stimpson 2023

Michael Stimpson has asserted his rights under the Copyright, Designs and
Patents Act 1988 to be identified as the author of this work.

British Library Cataloguing-in-Publication Data.
A catalogue record for this book is available from the British Library.

ISBN: 978-1-912421-55-8
Typeset by The City Press Leeds Ltd

Contents

Introduction

This book tells the stories of professional cricketers who were born in Oxford, or who have come from villages around the city, stretching back to the early days of the game up until the present era. Some influential professionals who came to live in Oxford are also included.

The book is not only about those Oxford men who have played the game professionally, but also covers some who have earned an income from being cricket groundsmen, coaches, practice bowlers, match promoters, and umpires, as well as inventors, makers and retailers of equipment. It is thus about Oxford's 'cricket professionals' in the widest sense of the term.

In concentrating on professionals, this book is not about cricket at Oxford University, but such is the strong academic influence over the city that University cricket does come in and out of the story.

The book also charts the development of the game of cricket in Oxford. The stories told will be of most interest to those from Oxford and Oxfordshire, and in reading it, some local knowledge will be an advantage. It is hoped that those from further afield, with an interest in cricket, will also find it worth reading.

The game of cricket is more than just about runs and wickets. It is full of stories and anecdotes about the people involved, some of which, about Oxford men, are told here.

Bullingdon Green and Cowley Marsh – Oxford's earliest cricket grounds

In 1644, the English Civil War was under way between the Royalists and Parliamentarians. King Charles I established Oxford as his headquarters, making good use of the hospitality from his supporters at the University. In May 1644, Roundhead forces came from Abingdon, forded the river at Sandford and then marched to the elevated part of Bullingdon Green, to view the city, before besieging it. Charles quickly fled Oxford, but later returned, which led to a couple more sieges of the city. Eventually, the Royalists lost Oxford to the Roundheads in 1646 and three years later Charles would lose his head.

So what has this to do with cricket? Well, the elevated spot on Bullingdon Green where the Roundhead army gathered to view the city in 1644 was later to become Oxford's first proper cricket ground.

In the 1600s, Bullingdon Green was an area of common land to the east of Oxford, lying between the villages of Temple Cowley, Horspath and Headington Quarry. At the end of Bullingdon Green nearest to the city, round about what are now the 5th and 6th holes of the Oxford golf course adjacent to Hollow Way, lay a flat elevated area, from which Parliamentary troops could get a good sight of Oxford. Years later, this ground also proved ideal for playing cricket.

Exactly when cricket began to be played on Bullingdon Green is not clear. At the time of Charles I, there are reports of cricket being played in the south coast counties of Sussex and Kent. Charles played real tennis when in Oxford and Oliver Cromwell later had a game of bowls in the city, but there is no record of anyone then playing cricket in or around Oxford.

It is known that cricket was being played at Oxford University in 1673, because that year a student named Thomas Salmon was publicly criticised for spending more time playing 'Trap and Cricket' than studying. Seeing more of sports fields than the inside of the library has remained a complaint from tutors about many students over the last 350 years.

Cricket continued to be played at Oxford University during the student days of the writer Dr Samuel Johnson, who came to Pembroke College in 1728. Very slowly the game developed in Oxford, with Bullingdon Green becoming the favoured cricket ground, despite the fact that it was a good horse ride from the city. There are references to the Gownsmen of the University playing on Bullingdon Green in 1763 and also the Gentlemen of the Oxford Cricket Club playing games there in 1765 and 1775. It is known that some matches took place on Port Meadow, to the north of the city, around this period.

Organised cricket in Oxford at this time was being played by well off gentlemen, for the most part. Occasionally the working men would get a look in, such as in 1764, when the gentlemen of the Wheatley club played a match against a team of domestic servants. Some of the gentry were not always good sports, because with Wheatley needing 39 to win this match, their last man refused to go in, which left the match, as well as all of the bets, undecided.

Around the 1770s, the Bullingdon Club was set up by some of the most wealthy and socially elite students at Oxford University. From the outset, this club concerned itself with drinking and dining, but on the sporting side, also made use of Bullingdon Green for games of cricket and horse riding. Presumably, the club took its name from the place where it held its sporting activities.

The Bullingdon Club became the prominent cricket side at Oxford University, whilst in London the Marylebone Club was formed in 1787, and it soon established itself as the premier cricket club in the country. The two clubs played each other on Bullingdon Green and at Lord's in 1795 and 1796.

Another area of common land to the east of Oxford known as Cowley Marsh also became used for cricket. A map of 1777 shows Cowley Marsh then extending from Temple Cowley down, on either side of the Cowley Road, to what is now Magdalen Road. The present Cowley Marsh Recreation Ground is thus only a small part of the original Cowley Marsh Common.

So, by the end of the 18th century, students and others from the city were travelling out to Cowley Marsh and Bullingdon Green to play games of cricket. This caused some friction with the locals of Cowley and in May 1797, a notice appeared in the *Oxford Journal*, stating that persons from Oxford and other places had been causing damage to Cowley Marsh and Bullingdon Green by playing cricket and other games on them. It warned that anyone trespassing on the commons without having obtained the permission of the parishioners of Cowley would be prosecuted!

Things clearly did not improve, as in September 1805 a similar notice appeared in the *Oxford Journal*, under the heading 'A CAUTION'. This again warned that anyone found playing cricket or other games on Cowley Marsh or Bullingdon Green without permission of the Commoners would be prosecuted. The names at the bottom of this notice were John White, John Hurst, William Hurst and Thomas King. These men were from prominent local farming families, who held commoner's rights over Bullingdon Green and Cowley Marsh, which enabled them to graze livestock on the common land.

Commoner's rights were attached to property ownership. As an example, a house in Church Cowley was advertised for sale in 1809, ownership of which included 'the right of common on Cowley Marsh for one horse, one cow, one sturk and ten sheep'. The wealthier in society, the property owners, were thus the main beneficiaries of these rights. The notice of 1805 seems to have done the trick and the students and other Oxonians playing on the commons probably placated the Cowley Commoners with a financial contribution.

The main cricket team in the city of Oxford at the start of the 1800s was from the Sociable Club, which was a gentlemen's club that met at the Alfred's Head Inn. It played some cricket at Port Meadow, against other teams of gentlemen from the city. Port Meadow was not very suitable for cricket as it was rough and uneven, as well as prone to flood: Bullingdon Green was a much better venue. In 1806, the Sociable Club played a combined team from 'Cowley and Iffley' at Bullingdon Green. The following year they played 'Cowley, Iffley, Littlemoor and neighbouring villages' at Bullingdon Green and despite the enlarged catchment area of the opposition, the Sociable Club still won by 125 runs.

The Bullingdon Club continued to play matches at Bullingdon Green, such as in June 1806, easily defeating a side of 11 gentlemen of Oxford, in May 1807 losing to Watlington, and in 1809 beating Wheatley. There were also many games against MCC, most of them ending in defeat. With the Napoleonic wars being fought between 1803 and 1815, the local Regiment of Oxford Loyal Volunteers also played matches on Bullingdon Green during this period, both amongst themselves and against such local sides as Wheatley.

By the last years of the 18th century and early 1800s most of the organised cricket was still being played by the better off members of society, such as the gentlemen in the Sociable Club, the posh students of the Bullingdon Club or even the officers of the Oxford Loyal Volunteers. The working men from the villages around Oxford just played games amongst themselves. In 1812, for example, there was a report of a match at Yarnton between 'eleven old married men' and 'eleven youths'.

If it was not possible to get teams together then single wicket matches were played, usually of one, two or three-a-side. Single wicket cricket had its own laws, which was necessary because of a lack of fielders. Runs could only be scored in front of the wicket as the ball was dead once it went behind the batsman's stumps. To score a single the batsman also had to run to the bowler's end and back again. Matches were often played for stakes, with many of the spectators betting on the outcome. In 1811, there was a report of a three-a-side match at Cowley Marsh between 'celebrated players of the city', with Mr Kensall and his sons taking on Messrs Knowles, Wilson and Pike.

In the early 1800s, a Cowley village team became established. This team was notable, as it seems that it was the first regular side in the Oxford area which was made up of largely working men. Every year Cowley would play at least one game against the City, and results showed that the Cowley villagers were more than a match for the cricketers from Oxford. In 1817, there was a two-day game at Bullingdon Green in which Cowley beat the City by 103 runs. A brief report of the game stated that 'The Cowley players having beaten Oxford twelve matches out of thirteen, have declined any future contest.'

The Bullingdon Club, as a representative team from the University, continued to play some prestigious fixtures. This culminated in a grand match at Bullingdon Green in June 1819 against 11 men of the County of Kent. This two-day match was played for an eye-watering stake of 550 guineas, and it was very close, with the Kent men winning by just four runs. The following month, the Bullingdon Club made the arduous journey down to Bromley to play a return match ... and lost again.

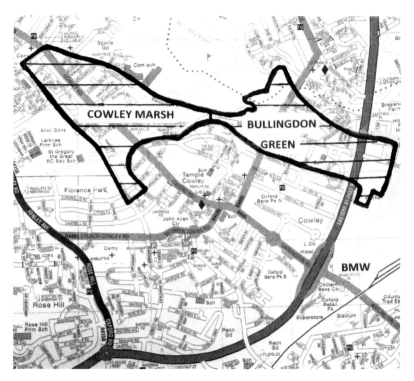

Cowley Marsh and Bullingdon Green.

A modern map of Cowley, with Cowley Marsh and Bullingdon Green shown hatched, as they existed in 1777. Both were then open commons, a good horse ride out of Oxford.

'That Singular Type of Humanity' – The Cowley professionals

The district of Cowley in the south-east of Oxford became well known in the 20th century for its motor car industry. Prior to that, many decades before the arrival of William Morris, Cowley was associated with something else.

The name of one of the few remaining pubs in Temple Cowley gives us a clue as to what Cowley was known for in the 19th century, as it is called 'The Cricketers Arms'. From the pre-Victorian times of the 1820s, for a period of over 100 years, Cowley had a production line of cricketers, rather than cars.

What we know today as Cowley was very different in the late 1700s. Back then, what was referred to as Cowley was actually three small communities, namely the village of Temple Cowley and the adjacent hamlets of Middle Cowley and Church Cowley. These three were then located well outside the boundaries of the city of Oxford and many of their inhabitants worked in agricultural jobs.

From the early 1800s onwards, some of the men of Cowley began to find a way of earning money from cricket-related jobs, as the game began to be played regularly on the nearby commons of Bullingdon Green and Cowley Marsh.

By the mid 1820s, a cricket club called the Magdalen Club had been formed for the best cricketers at the University, as opposed to those of expensive tastes and wild living in the Bullingdon Club. The story of why the University cricket club was called the Magdalen Club is rather long-winded. Apparently, Rev Henry Jenkins, who was Headmaster at the Magdalen College School for choir boys from 1810 to 1828, was a cricket enthusiast. He organised games of cricket for his boys, taking them down the Cowley Road to play on the nearest, and flattest, part of Cowley Marsh. Because of the schoolboys who played there, this cricket pitch became known as the Magdalen Ground. The site of this ground was at the corner of the junction of what is now Magdalen Road and Cowley Road, where housing and a large cinema were later built when the ground was sold off for development in the early 1930s.

Rev Jenkins apparently began renting the pitch and its surrounds, but when cricketers from the University became aware of it, they started playing there, with the Magdalen choir boys being moved over onto a corner of the ground. The University cricket club that was established took its name from the ground on which it played and so became the Magdalen Club.

Players from the Magdalen Club were selected for the Oxford University team that played the first ever match against Cambridge University, at Lord's in 1827. The next Varsity game was played at the Magdalen Ground on Cowley Marsh in 1829 and resulted in a home win for the Oxford men.

More and more cricket was being played on Cowley Marsh by the late 1820s and this created further employment opportunities for the local villagers. Working as groundsmen, practice bowlers or caterers were just some of the ways that the Cowley folk could make money out of cricket. The local children could also earn a halfpenny by retrieving cricket balls at practice sessions.

Writing in 1907, Thomas Case explained this in a uncomplimentary way, stating that the parishioners of Cowley had 'encouraged university men to go and play on the patches of the common, for the very good reason that they gave employment of a lucrative, if lazy, kind to a number of Cowley men and boys. Thus was gradually formed that singular type of humanity, well known to and bemoaned by Oxford cricketers – I mean the Cowley groundman and professional.'

A cricket match at the Magdalen Ground on Cowley Marsh in the 1820s.

Thomas Case had played cricket at the University and for Middlesex in the 1860s and then taught at various Oxford colleges. By the time he wrote these disparaging comments he had become the Professor of Metaphysical Philosophy at Oxford University. The parishioners of Cowley probably had very little knowledge of philosophy, but one thing that they did know was how to make a bob or two out of the likes of Thomas Case and his fellow cricketers from the University.

Another University man, Geoffrey Bolton, also wrote about 'loafers from Cowley' looking for and retrieving stray balls at the Magdalen Ground, during the practice sessions of the Magdalen Club. Amongst some academics, the men of Cowley certainly had a very poor reputation: but not everyone at the University looked down their noses at the Cowley professionals, some of whom, such as Peter Bancalari, were well liked.

Peter Bancalari – Not Just an Underhand Bowler

One of the first Cowley men to make a living out of cricket was an unlikely-sounding player named Pierre Bancalari. He had been born in Sardinia in 1806, but in a dramatic change of scenery, had moved to Cowley at a young age, with his parents and elder brother, Vincenzo. After leaving school he became a gamekeeper, but soon developed an interest in cricket and showed himself to be an accomplished underarm bowler (or underhand as it was called then) when playing in the Cowley team. All bowling in the 1820s was supposed to be underarm, although roundarm bowling was creeping in. Cricket was then a very different game from today as neither the batsmen nor wicketkeeper wore any pads or protective gloves.

In 1828, Pierre Bancalari started working for the Magdalen Club as a practice bowler on the Magdalen Ground. He was one of the first practice bowlers employed by the University, if not the very first.

Something of cricket at Oxford University in the 1830s is known from the writings of Rev James Pycroft, who played cricket for the University whilst at Trinity College from 1832 to 1836. Pycroft wrote, 'At this time professionals, either at the public schools or Universities were almost unknown. Cowley used to supply some useful bowlers, but all underhand. Such rustics as Hoskings, Blucher and Peter (short for Pieria Bancolari) were well-known names.'

Pycroft clearly had trouble spelling Bancalari's name. Around 1834 Pierre changed his first name to Peter, which was easier for the locals to both pronounce and spell.

During the 1830s, as well as working for the University as a practice bowler, Peter Bancalari made money by playing single wicket matches on Cowley Marsh for stakes. In July

1837, as an example, Bancalari and Charlie Hodgkins defeated a pair of Oxford City cricketers, in a two-day game. A couple of months later Bancalari showed that he was also a useful batsman, when he and Hodgkins won a match against another two leading Oxford City players. The Oxford pair could only muster a total of 25 runs in their two innings, whereas Hodgkins (16) and Bancalari (24) made 40 in their only innings, to win easily.

Bancalari also became part of a formidable Cowley team, who were always keen to play matches for stakes. In 1834, Cowley played a game on Bullingdon Green against the Oxford Albion Club for 22 guineas, which the Cowley men won. In 1837, after beating a team of Oxford players, a notice soon appeared in the *Oxford Gazette*, reading, 'The Cowley Village Club are open to play the Eleven from Oxford, with whom they contended on Tuesday last, for any sum from £1 to £5 each man.' Cowley travelled to Great Milton in 1839 and won a game that was played for 11 guineas a side. A return match was to have been played on Bullingdon Green, but Great Milton backed out of this and forfeited their stakes. Great Milton decided to have a match against Little Milton instead, for a more affordable £2 15s a side.

Cowley did not always have its own way. When beaten by the University in 1835, the Cowley team was bowled out for 63 in its first innings, but Bancalari did manage to score an undefeated 17, the only man to reach double figures. Playing for stakes and having a steady income as a practice bowler for the University provided Peter with healthy summer earnings.

There was a regular Town v University fixture in the 1830s and Peter played against the students in these games. Big crowds would come to watch these matches at Cowley Marsh, as they would when the University played its most prestigious annual fixture against MCC.

In 1835, a new MCC law legitimised roundarm bowling. Under this law, the ball had to be bowled with the hand not above the shoulder at the point of delivery. Considerable pace could be generated with this now legal slinging, roundarm action.

With roundarm bowling given official approval, leg guards and batting gloves were developed in the 1840s, to give batsmen some protection. The bowlers did not have it all their own way though, as bat design had been improved in the 1830s with the development of separate spliced handles, which were then given extra spring by the insertion of whalebone or even steel.

Peter Bancalari recognised the increasing demand for cricket equipment and with some colleges laying out grounds on Bullingdon Green and Cowley Marsh in the 1840s he began selling kit from premises on the Cowley Road.

As he got older and his underarm bowling went out of fashion, Bancalari switched to umpiring. He became a main umpire for the University team, officiating in many of their matches on the Magdalen Ground from the late 1840s through to the 1860s. Three Varsity matches were played at the Magdalen Ground, in 1846, 1848 and 1850 (all resulting in home wins), but it is not known whether Bancalari umpired in these games. After that, Lord's became the regular venue.

Bancalari did a lot of umpiring, whether it was for University matches and practice games, or for college sides. As his reputation grew, he was also asked to umpire other big matches in the county, such as when Banbury played a grand match against the All-England Eleven in 1852.

In a game that Peter probably umpired at the Magdalen Ground in 1853, there was some sensational bowling, as well as an umpiring error which facilitated the setting of a unique record. Back then, there were just four balls in an over, but the Oxford University bowler Arthur Cazenove managed to take five wickets in one over, in a game against an Oxfordshire team. This seemingly impossible feat was due to the umpire miscounting and allowing an extra fifth delivery. Cazenove took all ten wickets in the innings, so had a tremendous day ... unlike the umpire! Whether it was Peter Bancalari or another umpire who miscounted is not known.

As well as umpiring, Peter also did other odd jobs around the Magdalen Ground. In the days before there was a pavilion, tents would be erected for matches, and he was paid to put them up. For two-day or three-day matches, the tents would be left up for the duration of the game and having umpired all day, Peter would then earn some extra money for 'sitting up' in the tents overnight, to ensure that they were still there in the morning. His sleepless nights came to an end in 1856, when a new brick pavilion was built on the Magdalen Ground, a major benefit of which was that it had toilets.

By 1860, Bancalari's business was going well, and he moved to larger premises, the Cricket Depot, on Cowley Road. By then he had become a well-known personality in the cricketing world of Oxford and would sometimes get his own team together. In July 1860, there was a game involving many old Cowley cricketers when Peter Bancalari's Eleven played John Hurst's Eleven on the Magdalen Ground. As if he was not already busy enough, by 1863 he had also become the groundsman at Magdalen College School. Later in life, Bancalari also started making some cricket bats, as well as selling them.

Peter Bancalari died in 1869, at the age of 63. He had no children and so what was then called his Cricket and Athletic Depot was taken over by a nephew, and it continued to thrive for many years. Bancalari started as an underarm bowler, a style used from the earliest days, but during his life in cricket, he saw dramatic change as the game transformed into something close to what we know today.

Bancalari was much more than just a bowler, as he led the way for local Oxford cricket professionals. Apart from being one of the first practice bowlers employed by the University, he was also a prominent early professional umpire and one of the first local cricket equipment retailers. A large part of his success was probably due to the fact that, whatever he did, he was well-liked and respected. Everyone seemed to have a good word to say for Peter. The University cricketers thought so much of him that they organised a two-day testimonial match for his benefit in 1850, between graduates and undergraduates. This was one of the first benefit games for a University employee and showed that there were many student cricketers who did not share Thomas Case's jaundiced views of Cowley professionals.

In the account books of the Magdalen Club, payments to such people as 'Hodgkins the groundsman' were noted using their surname. In contrast, payments to Peter were sometimes recorded using his first name only, which shows remarkable familiarity and illustrates how well he was thought of. The social gap between University students and Peter Bancalari was wide, but at the cricket ground there was a common bond between them.

There is a quaint story told by James Pycroft, which reflects Peter Bancalari's feeling of loyalty to the University cricketers. In an important University game against MCC in 1837, Bancalari was fielding as a substitute for the MCC player Mr Ben Aislabie. He was positioned on the boundary when, with the last pair at the wicket, the University batsman F Wright hit the ball high in the air, passing just over Bancalari's head. Pycroft later said to him 'Peter, if you had been a foot taller you would have caught that ball.' 'No, I shouldn't, sir,' was the reply. 'I was fielding for Mr Aislabie and he couldn't have caught nothing; then why should I? No sir, I would not catch Mr Wright out to please the Marylebone gentlemen, nor nobody.'

Bancalari was correct in thinking that Mr Ben Aislabie would have struggled to take a difficult catch on the boundary, as he was a large man of about twenty stones, whose presence on the cricket field was once described as being like 'a hippopotamus among greyhounds'. When the ball went up in the air, Peter Bancalari's loyalties lay firmly with the University cricketers that paid him!

Cricketing Antiques

There is a very old cricket bat on display in a museum in Sevenoaks, which might have been owned, or even used, by Peter Bancalari. The bat was apparently made about 1755, by William Pett of Sevenoaks, and is one of the oldest surviving cricket bats. It is now black, due it seems to many coats of preservative, but the handle has been re-bound with cord and on one side it is stamped with the name 'Bancalari'. It is an unspliced bat, of the type that would have been in use when Peter Bancalari first played cricket.

It is known that this bat spent some time in Oxford, as it was on show in the shop window of Turner Brothers, the Oxford cricket and tennis outfitters, in the 1930s.

Could Peter Bancalari have used this this old bat? Perhaps, but probably unlikely, given that it would already have been something of a relic by the time he was playing. It is more likely that the bat was given a new cord grip at Bancalari's Cricket Depot and the name then stamped on it. Even so, it is fitting that the name of Oxford's first prominent cricket professional is on this vintage bat.

Another fine piece of cricketing history is a painted lithograph, dating from 1850, which is on display in Vincent's Club, in Oxford. This lithograph is titled 'An Old Servant to the Magdalen Cricket Club' and shows an unnamed, well-dressed man stood in a doorway, holding a cricket bat (see the following page).

This man is almost certainly Peter Bancalari. There are some cricket bats shown in the window at the side of the picture. Bancalari was a cricket retailer and it would make sense that there would be some cricket bats in his shop window. Everything points to the man in the picture being Peter Bancalari.

The lithograph was probably produced to mark the benefit

given to Peter Bancalari by the University cricketers in 1850. Its commissioning again shows the high esteem in which he was held.

Peter Bancalari 1806 - 1869

'An Old Servant to the Magdalen Club' Peter Bancalari?

Cricketing Farmers – The Hurst Brothers

In 1843, the Oxford University team that played against MCC at Lord's included the three brothers, Richard, John and Edward Hurst. What is strange about this is that the brothers were not students at the University but were farmers from Cowley. How they came to be playing for the University at Lord's is a mystery. The match was at the end of June, so perhaps the University team was short of players because some students had already returned home. Whatever the reason, the farming Hurst brothers must have had a high social standing in order to be selected as guests for Oxford University.

This was to be the only first-class match that the Hurst brothers would ever play. Richard and Edward were batsmen, but unfortunately they only scored 30 runs between them in this game. John was a fast bowler and he put in an impressive bowling performance at Lord's, taking six wickets in MCC's first innings and another five in the second. His bowling record in first-class cricket is thus 11 wickets at an average of about five apiece! It was a low scoring game and the pitch at Lord's was not of a high standard. It compared unfavourably with the Magdalen Ground on Cowley Marsh, according to the Oxford men.

The Hurst brothers came from an old-established farming family in Cowley and they went on to farm large swathes of land to the east of Oxford. They were close in age, with Edward born in 1816, John in 1817 and Richard a year later. By 1834, despite their youth, Edward and John were playing for the Cowley club. Younger brother Richard soon joined them in the Cowley team, which by 1840 had become a formidable side.

In many villages around Oxford, farmers were an important element in the development of cricket in this era, as they owned land on which games could be played, had the money to buy equipment and could give their workers time off to play the game, if they were feeling generous. So it was in Cowley, as the Hurst family became the backbone of the club, helping to organise and fund it, as well as give it some respectability.

At the annual dinner of Cowley CC in 1840, which was held at the Royal Oak, Middle Cowley, Edward Hurst, the Chairman, reported that the club had won every game that season and that 'The acknowledged superiority of the Cowley players had induced many gentlemen to become honorary members.' Cowley was certainly going up in the world if gentlemen from the upper classes wanted to be associated with its cricket club, the majority of whose players were working men.

Throughout the 1840s, Cowley continued to be the strongest club side in the Oxford area. There were regular matches against the University which attracted a lot of interest and were keenly contested. A report in the *Oxford Journal* from May 1843 suggests that the Cowley players were not short of self-confidence, as it stated, 'The University of Oxford played a match with the village of Cowley, on Monday and Friday last, when contrary to their expectations, the latter were defeated by 17 runs.' No matter, when the two sides met again the following month, Cowley was the victor.

The Cowley team also had an annual game against the rest of Oxford and very rarely was Cowley beaten in this fixture. Cowley even had a match against MCC in 1840, quite remarkable for a small village team to take on the most prominent cricket club in the country! In 1849 Cowley played against 11 Players and Gentlemen of Oxfordshire and won by an innings.

When Cowley played the University in a two-innings match at Cowley Marsh in 1844, there were four Hursts in the Cowley side, as the three brothers had been joined by their cousin James. Despite a first-innings lead, Cowley slipped to a defeat due to some poor fielding, but John Hurst took at least nine wickets in the match. He was clearly a threat with a ball in his hand, one report referring to his 'fine slashing bowling'.

In the same year, there was an attempt to form an Oxfordshire County Cricket Club, but after initial enthusiasm nothing came of this. An unofficial county side called the Bullingdon Union did have some matches and all three Hurst brothers played for this team. There were two games against a Berkshire side in 1847, with Edward Hurst top-scoring in both innings of the home match.

The Hurst brothers continued to play in Cowley's big matches over the next few seasons. Richard Hurst also opened the batting for a 16-man Oxfordshire team that played an All-England Eleven in 1851 and he was one of only two local Oxford men (the rest were from the University) in Oxfordshire sides that played against Fuller Pilch's England Eleven in 1852 and 1853.

By the mid 1850s, it seems that the three Hurst brothers had stopped playing for Cowley and had joined the more refined Oxford City club. Edward Hurst farmed land on Bullingdon Green, which included the old cricket ground, and in 1856 he hosted a match there between a county team selected by himself, against a side from the city, which was picked by William Bacon. He continued to organise matches at Bullingdon Green and was a convivial host. In a Cowley v Borough match in 1863, it was reported that John Hurst provided the lunch, dinner and drinks for a large party of players and spectators. He could afford this, as by this time the brothers were well off, farming over 650 acres between them and employing a large number of men and boys. Various members of the family, including the three brothers, owned a large part of the farmland between Temple Cowley and Magdalen Bridge and they increased their wealth by selling off this land for housing development in the 1850s and 1860s.

All three of the Hurst brothers were to die in their 50s,

and there was an unhappy ending to the life of John Hurst. In early March 1868, the *Oxford Times* reported, under the heading 'SAD OCCURRENCE AT TEMPLE COWLEY':

> The general quietude of this little village was greatly disturbed on Wednesday morning last, when the report got about that one of its chief and most respected inhabitants (Mr John Hurst, farmer) had put an end to his existence by blowing his brains out. Mr Hurst was a genial companion and large-hearted neighbour, and when the sad occurrence became generally known in Cowley and its neighbourhood, a feeling of sorrow was universally felt and expressed.

A sad occurrence indeed.

The Hurst brothers were an important element in establishing Cowley as a cricketing force between the 1830s and 1850s. Due to their generosity, organisation and influence, they helped cricket to flourish in Cowley, making a large contribution both on and off the field. The cricket professionals who came out of Cowley during this period had a lot to be thankful to the Hursts. After the brothers left, the Cowley club went into decline and folded for a period in the 1860s.

These days, the Hurst family is still remembered by a street named after them in the east of Oxford.

Edward Hurst 1816 - 1866

John Hurst 1817 - 1868

Richard Hurst 1818 - 1873

David Burrin – Fast Roundarm Bowler for Hire

Cricket began in England as a working man's game, with rough and ready matches played amongst themselves. It was then taken up by the upper classes, who played the game for sport, for enjoyment, and often for a wager on the side. When the size of either the wager or the egos of those involved increased and the need to win was heightened, they started to hire the best cricketers from the labouring classes to play for them. In a nutshell, this is how two types of English cricketer developed: the 'Gentleman' (amateur) and the 'Player' (professional).

In 1806, the first Gentlemen v Players match took place. By the 1840s, well before the days of Test matches, it had become established as an important annual fixture, which was usually played at Lord's. This fixture was mimicked in Oxford when an annual Gentlemen v Players match began to be played at Cowley Marsh in the 1840s, between Gentlemen (mostly from the University) and Players (those employed on the cricket grounds at Cowley Marsh and Bullingdon Green). A strong team of professionals could be fielded from the groundsmen and practice bowlers working at these grounds. Two of the best of the professionals were the Burrin brothers.

William and David Burrin were from a Cowley family. They did not have an easy life when they were young, as they had a blind elder sister, and their father spent some time in jail for stealing lead. Growing up, the boys followed their father into the masonry trade, but from a young age made a name for themselves as cricketers.

William Burrin began playing for the strong Cowley team in 1840, when he was only 16 years old. He was a left-arm bowler and played regularly for Cowley over the next few seasons. He must have been good, as in 1843 he was selected to play as a guest professional for Oxford University against

MCC at Lord's.

By 1846, William Burrin had been joined in the Cowley side by his younger brother David, who was a fast roundarm bowler. The brothers were both selected for Bullingdon Union, the unofficial Oxfordshire team, to play against Berkshire in 1847. They also began to earn money by playing as guests for other clubs, such as when they appeared for Adderbury, then a prominent club in the north of the county, in a two-day match against Northampton in 1847.

The Burrin brothers became a fearsome opening bowling combination and many college and other local teams that played against Cowley suffered at their hands. In 1848, Cowley beat Wadham College in a two-innings match, with the Burrin brothers taking nine wickets between them in Wadham's second innings, the other being a run out: 'The splendid bowling of the two Burrins ... was the admiration of the whole field,' commented a match report. The same year David Burrin took eight wickets as Oxford City was bowled out for 67 when losing to Cowley.

By 1849, David had surpassed his brother and one of his finest bowling performances was taking ten wickets for Cowley in a two-innings match when an Oxfordshire team was easily beaten. When a big game was organised for an Oxfordshire XVI to play against Kent that season, David Burrin was selected for the home side. Kent had been the leading county team over the previous decade or so and their side included some of the most well-known cricketers in the country. With the help of having 16 players in the field, David Burrin took seven wickets in the match, as Oxfordshire triumphed.

The following season, David Burrin was again in fine form, taking 15 wickets in a Town v University match in May. The next month, he was selected for an Oxfordshire team of 18 to play a match against an All-England Eleven in Oxford.

This All-England Eleven had been set up in 1846 by William Clarke, a professional bowler from Nottingham, who had moved down to work at the Marylebone Club. Clarke was unhappy with his limited remuneration at Lord's and so he formed his own 'England' team, made up of many of the best professional players in the country. His All-England side travelled around the country playing games against local clubs and county teams, who might have up to 22 players to even things up. With famous cricketers in his side, the All-England Eleven was popular wherever it went. Clarke would demand a fee of about £70 for his team to play a match, although sometimes he would opt to take the gate money instead, out of which he paid his players anything between £3 to £6 a game. At its peak in 1851 the All-England team played 34 matches, so its professional players earned a lot of money, whilst Clarke made a small fortune!

When it came to play in Oxford in 1850, the All-England Eleven was beaten by the 18 men of Oxfordshire, as David Burrin took a ten-wicket haul in the match, with some of the best batsmen in the country included in his victims. 'The bowling of Burrin and Mr Willis was quite equal, if not superior to that of All-England,' stated a report. By now David Burrin's reputation was spreading and later that summer he was taken on by the Reading club as their professional.

David Burrin again bowled well when 16 of Oxfordshire played the All-England Eleven in a rain-affected match in 1851. Ambitiously, the Banbury club also had a match against the All-England team that season, but to help them along, Banbury was allowed to have 22 players, which included two professional bowlers, one being David Burrin. The two pros, Bickley and Burrin, took all of the wickets for Banbury, apart from a run-out, as the town side surprisingly won a low-scoring game.

Having impressed in Oxford and Reading, over the following couple of seasons Burrin was recruited by Berkshire clubs such as Hungerford Park and Maidenhead to play as a hired hand against the All-England Eleven and an equally strong breakaway side called the United All-England Eleven. He bowled particularly well for Hungerford in 1852, when the All-England team crumbled to just 12 all out in its first innings, with organiser William Clarke included in Burrin's victims. In the same fixture the following year he twice dismissed Clarke, as he took 11 England wickets in the match.

By 1854, David Burrin had become known throughout the country and he was recruited by such clubs as Rugby, Liverpool, Broughton, Northampton, and Rotherham to play for them in matches against the travelling England sides, taking plenty of wickets in doing so. The quality of his bowling is illustrated by the fact that in the eight games that he played against All-England, he dismissed George Parr, who was then the leading batsman in the country, eight times. No batsman in the land was comfortable facing the bowling of David Burrin.

Back home in Cowley, William and David Burrin fell out with their home club. In August 1851, playing for Cowley against Brackley, the Burrin brothers took many wickets, but it seems they voiced their displeasure with the standard of the fielding of their team-mates. A report of the match finished with the comment that, 'We understand the Cowley side were very much dissatisfied with the conduct of the Burrins and that several of them expressed their determination never to enter the field again with them.' It seems that following the Brackley game, the Burrin brothers did not play for Cowley again.

After 1854, David Burrin stopped travelling long distances to play matches. Nevertheless, he was still prepared to journey to neighbouring counties, and he played for Reading against the All-England Eleven in 1855. That year he turned out as a professional guest for many local gentlemen's sides, including such diverse teams as Frilford, the Barristers of Oxford, and Wheatley South Oxfordshire. He was also persuaded to play for Moreton-in-Marsh in a two-day fixture against Oxford Harlequins, at which it was reported that 'A small admission fee to the ground was charged each day, which kept the company select and orderly.' In that part of Gloucestershire, it seems that gate money was not seen as a means of making money, but as a novel way of keeping out the 'riff-raff'!

For whatever reason, whether injury or other commitments perhaps, in the late 1850s Burrin confined his guest professional appearances nearer to home. If any local team needed a fast bowler, David Burrin was still happy to oblige ... for a payment of course. As in earlier years, he worked on the grounds at Bullingdon Green and he appeared in some matches as a professional guest for the Bullingdon Club: a lowly builder taking the field in the same team as such aristocrats as the Marquis of Bowmont!

When it came to county cricket, Burrin was not selected for the official Oxfordshire CCC that was briefly in existence in 1856 and 1857. It seems that he could be an abrasive character and perhaps he had ruffled a few too many feathers by then.

David Burrin had turned out as a guest professional for the Gentlemen of Buckinghamshire against the Gentlemen of Berkshire in 1849, earning his money by taking nine wickets as Berkshire was bowled out for 99. Eight years later, he changed sides, when he played as a professional guest for the Gentlemen of Berkshire against the Buckinghamshire Gents. When there was money to be earned, there was no such thing as loyalty and the hard-headed professional cricketer of this era would play for whoever paid him.

With his cricket still going well, David Burrin gave up masonry, and combined playing with working as a professional at the Oriel College and Balliol College cricket grounds, as well as running a beer house.

Tragically, David Burrin died in 1863 in Temple Cowley, at the age of just 36. In his brief life, he had left his mark on the game of cricket, for he had been a devastating bowler, capable of dismissing the best batsmen of the day, as well as terrorising many local and University cricketers.

The year after Burrin died, overarm bowling, as we know it today, was legalised. David Burrin was thus one of the last exponents of roundarm bowling and as far as Oxford is concerned, he was the finest.

William Burrin also became a pub landlord in Temple Cowley. Like his father, he had a few scrapes with the law, as he was not averse to having a fight, sometimes forgot to pay his rates and was prosecuted for both serving after hours and also using undersized beer cups. He died at Temple Cowley in 1875, at the age of 52, leaving his widow Harriett to take over as landlady of their beer house, the Bullingdon Arms.

David Burrin 1827 - 1863

William Burrin 1824 - 1875

Edward Martin and Tom Nixon –
Entrepreneur and Inventor

The University initially opposed the idea of the railway coming to Oxford (there was a fear that it would be too easy for students to go off socialising in London), but eventually Brunel built a line from Didcot to Oxford, which he came to open in 1844. The railway line ran up from the south of the city, parallel to the Abingdon Road, along what is now Marlborough Road, and a station was built just south of the river, at the end of Western Road.

With a new railway station located close to the centre of Oxford, a Kent cricketer named Edward Martin spotted an opportunity. He came to Oxford in 1848 and rented a field from Brasenose College behind the Old White House Inn, on the Abingdon Road. Martin set about creating a cricket ground on this field, which was only a good cricket ball's throw from the new Great Western Railway station, an ideal location for attracting spectators from the countryside and beyond, as well as making it easy for cricketers to travel to the city. To give it some grandeur, he named this new cricket ground after the Prince of Wales.

Martin's new ground was a commercial venture in partnership with the famous Kent batsman Fuller Pilch, with whom he also collaborated in bat making at premises in St Aldates, in the city centre. Pilch had been the best batsman in the country in the 1830s and early 1840s. It was a shrewd move by Martin to use both Pilch's name and money in their business.

Edward Martin had been born in a small village in Kent, in 1814, and was from a family which had a cricket ball manufacturing business. He initially played as a professional for Hampshire and Dorset sides, as well as various clubs in the south, including West of England in Bath. In 1845, at the age of 30, Martin began playing for the Kent team, which had been the strongest county side in England for a few years. Martin was a 'free hard hitter' and a 'most excellent field, especially at long leg', according to Pycroft. Having played for Kent for three seasons, Martin did not appear for them in 1848, because he went up to be a professional for the Manchester club that summer, but after that he managed to turn out for Kent in a few more matches up until 1851.

Back in Oxford, Martin's plan was to organise big matches on his cricket ground, which would draw in large crowds and make him a good income. Initially he wanted to arrange a match between Oxford University and Kent at his new ground, but the University cricketing hierarchy 'poured cold water' on the idea. Undeterred, Martin turned to local Oxford cricketers, some of whom were professionals, and together with 'seven gentlemen of the University, who were not quite so fastidious as some others of that body', he formed an Oxfordshire team of 16 to take on the mighty Kent team. A two-day 'Grand Match' was played between these sides in May 1849, at Martin's ground, with the Kent team including the two of the best-known English cricketers of that era, batsman Fuller Pilch and allrounder Alfred Mynn, who have been described as the Geoffrey Boycott and Ian Botham of their time. Nothing like it had been seen in Oxford before. In previous years the University had played important matches against such teams as the Marylebone Club at Cowley Marsh, but these had never generated the public excitement of the Kent match.

The game was evenly poised, until Kent collapsed to 36 all out in its second innings. As previously recounted, the young Cowley roundarmer David Burrin bowled well and took wickets, as Fuller Pilch, with an undefeated 16, was the only Kent batsman to reach double figures. Edward Martin played for Kent in this big game, but failed to score in both innings, as Oxfordshire won. There was a good-sized crowd on both days and with an admission charge of either 1s or 6d, the match was a financial success for Martin. He went on to organise other lower-profile games on his ground that season, as well as some single wicket matches.

Emboldened by the success of the Kent match, the following year Martin arranged a game between William Clarke's All-England Eleven and 18 of Oxfordshire, at his Prince of Wales ground. Edward Martin had previously played against the All-England Eleven and could see that it would be a great attraction in Oxford. The match was well-supported, and the local spectators must have been surprised to see Oxfordshire win convincingly by 187 runs.

A drawback of Martin's cricket ground was that its small size limited the number of spectators. He could not find a local side of any stature to play there regularly and the building of a new, much larger, Christ Church cricket ground close by seems to have scuppered Martin's plans to make his the premier cricket ground in the city. It was a case of 'if you cannot beat them, join them', and Martin became the head groundsman of the new Christ Church ground. After 1850, there were to be no more grand matches played on the Prince of Wales Ground.

In 1848, the same year that Edward Martin had come to Oxford, an enterprising local cricketer named Frank Fenner opened his own cricket ground in Cambridge. Clubs from the university, county and town all played on Frank's ground, and it remains as Cambridge University's home pitch to this day. Fenner's cricket ground was a success, unfortunately Martin's was not.

In 1851, when the All-England Eleven returned to play 16 of Oxfordshire, it was at the new Christ Church ground, as it was the following year when Fuller Pilch's All-England Eleven played Oxfordshire. Bad weather ruined this match, which meant that Martin and Pilch, the organisers, lost money. Oxfordshire played a Fuller Pilch England team again in 1853, but after that it was University sides that would play England teams at Christ Church, Cowley Marsh and Lord's.

The building of a new Oxford railway station (on its present site, to the west of the city centre) meant that the GWR station near to the Prince of Wales ground was closed to passengers in October 1852. This was the final blow for Martin's aspirations of creating a profitable, top-class cricket ground.

Martin's business partnership with Fuller Pilch was officially dissolved in 1855 but he continued to make bats on his own. One type of bat that he produced had been designed by a cricketer with an inventive mind named Thomas Nixon.

Tom Nixon had made his name as a slow roundarm spin bowler when playing for the County of Nottingham, before becoming a professional at Lord's in 1851. That year he started playing for All-England, before joining the breakaway United All-England team the following season. He would also sometimes play against England sides for local teams who needed the assistance of a professional bowler. He was willing to travel the country playing as a professional for clubs that needed a good bowler and he also played for MCC, where he began to earn a reputation as a knowledgeable coach. From 1853 onwards Nixon began umpiring top matches at Lord's, so with all of this, he was very busy.

In 1853, Nixon came to Oxford as a college professional and turned out for the Players side in the annual match against the University, taking 12 wickets, as the professionals were victorious. In June 1855, he played for an England Eleven selected by Martin and Pilch against 22 of Christ Church. He took 15 wickets in the game and later that year came to live permanently in the city.

Tom Nixon was ingenious and came up with ideas for all sorts of innovative cricket equipment. He led the way in improving the design of leg guards for batsmen. In early days, batsmen had used rolled-up socks or shin padding to give them protection but with the advent of fast roundarm bowling something more substantial was needed. Nixon initially designed some batting pads using cork, but after living in Oxford for a few months, he got together with Edward Martin to produce a new lightweight leg guard. His 'open leg guards' used cane and were marketed as being cooler and lighter than any others, whilst still giving protection against the fastest of bowling. Martin sold them for 15s a pair, and this type of pad went on to be used for a long time.

Tom Nixon also created a cane-handled cricket bat (previously willow or ash had been used). The idea of having a handle made entirely of cane was that it would give more spring to the blade. He again teamed up with Edward Martin, who produced and sold this bat, but it had some teething problems as the cane handle was prone to break.

In 1856 Nixon took over the Prince of Wales Ground and also succeeded Edward Martin as the landlord of the adjacent Old White House Inn. He started working as a practice bowler at the Christ Church cricket ground and over the next few years played for Christ Church as a professional guest in many of their big matches, the most prominent of which were against England teams.

Nixon was involved in setting up a new Oxfordshire CCC in 1856, perhaps hoping that the county side would play at his Prince of Wales Ground. Despite talk of fixtures against other counties such as Sussex and Warwickshire, in the event only four Oxfordshire games were played over the next two seasons, all of them against Surrey, and all ending in defeat. Playing as a professional for Oxfordshire in three of these matches, Nixon earned his match fees by taking a total of 23 wickets. Edward Martin also played in the first two games against Surrey and made a contribution with some aggressive batting.

The Oxfordshire teams that were selected against Surrey were not representative of the county, as they included mostly University players. Early enthusiasm for the county club soon cooled and it folded in 1857. It would be another 134 years before Oxfordshire once more played Surrey: in 1991, Surrey won again, in a bowl-out at the Oval, after the original National Westminster Bank Trophy game had been rained off.

To generate some income, Tom Nixon organised fireworks displays and athletics events on the Prince of Wales Ground. One popular event in October 1856 involved James Pudney attempting to run 11 miles in an hour. A large crowd came to watch this event and there was drama when Pudney crossed the finishing line, as it could not be decided whether he had finished one second under or one second over an hour, because of disputes about stopwatches! On the cricketing front, Nixon arranged for the new South Oxford club to play at his White House Ground, as it had then become known.

Although living in Oxford, Tom Nixon continued to play all around the country over the next few seasons, as well as in some big games at home. In 1859, when the United All-England Eleven played a match at the Christ Church cricket ground against '18 Gentlemen of Christ Church and two Players', Nixon again showed his worth, taking five wickets in England's first innings. As in previous years, Edward Martin presented one of Nixon's cane-handled bats to the highest scorer on the Christ Church side.

Meanwhile, Edward Martin got into trouble for speaking his mind. In November 1859 he appeared in court charged with using 'abusive and insulting language'. His ire was directed at a builder who he thought was swindling ratepayers. He was fined 40s with 8s costs, which he paid immediately.

The Prince of Wales came to Oxford in October 1859 to enrol as a student at Christ Church. How much studying he did can only be speculated, but he was a cricket enthusiast, and the following summer had a series of private coaching sessions with the Christ Church head groundsman, Edward Martin. Presumably it was a coincidence that just over a decade earlier, Martin had named the new cricket ground that he created after the Prince of Wales.

As well as coaching, Edward Martin had fingers in other pies. By 1860 he was still making cricket bats at his premises in St Aldates, from where he also sold other cricket equipment. He also had 13 acres of land to the south of the city, on which he kept horses, and was still the head groundsman at the Christ Church cricket ground. The last time that Martin was in the news in Oxford was in December 1860, when a gate on the Christ Church ground had been left open one evening and two of his horses were killed when they wandered from the ground onto the adjoining railway line.

Sometime in the early part of 1861, Edward Martin left Oxford. It seems that he went in a hurry, leaving behind his wife and two small children, who continued to live in the city. He also left a large amount of unsold cricket equipment. Whatever the reason for Martin's departure, no one seemed to know much about it. Martin 'absconded in a very mysterious manner', according to the *Oxford Chronicle and Reading Gazette*, leaving Christ Church with no head groundsman.

James Pycroft gave some interesting information about Martin's disappearance in his *Oxford Memories* book, which was published some 25 years later. According to Pycroft, when Martin was living in Oxford, he had struck up a friendship with a 'wealthy collegian'. This friend apparently gave Martin a farm at Leominster, which he later sold for 'several hundreds of pounds'. One morning, with the proceeds of the sale in his pocket, Martin left his Oxford home on a favourite horse and 'nothing more was ever heard of him'.

The tale of Martin acquiring a farm is given some credence by the fact that when the 1861 census was taken in April of that year, shortly after he had disappeared, his wife Eliza gave her occupation as 'farmers wife'. She lived nowhere near a farm, however, as her home was in the centre of Oxford, where she stayed for the rest of her life.

It was widely assumed that Martin had probably been robbed and murdered. After about a year's absence, it was accepted that he was not coming back to Oxford, and in May 1862 a special sale was held of the stock of new cricket equipment at his business, including 500 bats. Nothing was ever heard of what had happened to Martin until November 1869, when there was some astonishing news. A man who had been killed when falling from his horse as he was returning from a hunt near Lewes in Sussex was identified by papers in his house as being Edward Martin. He had managed to live anonymously for nearly nine years, having cut all contacts with his family and friends, as well as the cricketing world. This must have come as a tremendous shock to his wife and children. All very mysterious!

Meanwhile, back in Kent, the Martin family cricket ball manufacturing business in the village of Teston ran into financial difficulties and in 1871 it was bought by Alfred Reader, who was the local shopkeeper and postmaster. Under Alfred Reader, the firm prospered and became a competitor to the well-known Duke and Twort companies. Alfred Reader went on to become a famous brand in the world of cricket balls and remains prominent today, although now owned by Kookaburra.

As for Tom Nixon, he continued inventing. In 1862, he patented a new bowling machine which was based on the design of an ancient Greek siege weapon. Nixon moved up to Cheshire around this time, but he would sometimes return to Oxford. Tom had become a knowledgeable groundsman and he was employed by Merton College to convert a field into their cricket ground over the winter of 1865/66. He was given a benefit game by MCC in 1867 for his service as a ground bowler and umpire, and by then he had opened a cricket equipment business in Cheshire, doubtless selling some of the items that he had invented.

So Thomas Nixon and Edward Martin were briefly influential figures in the cricketing world of Oxford. Martin was an entrepreneur who first brought the glamour of England teams to play matches in the city. He was a wheeler-dealer character, not entirely trustworthy, with an eye for making money. Martin's most lasting contribution to sport in the city was the creation of a cricket ground, which became known as the White House ground and was taken over by Oxford City FC in 1900 as their home football pitch. The University often has the final say on things in Oxford and sadly, Brasenose College evicted Oxford City in 1988, closed the football ground and developed it with housing.

Tom Nixon, An Inventive Spin Bowler.

Tom Nixon was a cricketing allrounder. As well as being a fine bowler, coach, umpire and groundsman, he also helped to get a new Oxfordshire CCC off the ground, but Tom Nixon's biggest contribution to the game of cricket was the innovative equipment that he designed. In particular, he improved the design of batting pads, close to something that we know today, and this had a profound effect on the way that the game would be played from then on. Once they had a good pair of pads on their legs, batsmen had no excuse for backing away and not getting into line with the ball!

Thomas Nixon 1815 - 1877
First-class 54 matches
264 wickets @ 10.0

Edward Martin 1814 - 1869
First-class 41 matches
682 runs @ 9.3

The Longest Hit

Edward Martin was a skilled bat maker and a shrewd businessman, but not the most honest of men. All three of these traits were illustrated in his involvement with a remarkable event that was reported to have taken place on a cricket ground in Oxford in 1856.

With the advent of Twenty20 cricket and the Hundred, the sight of batsmen hitting sixes into and over the stands has become commonplace. With thick, springy bats, even mishits can fly off for a six nowadays. Boundaries are often quite short in the modern limited-over game and can be cleared with ease. But exactly how far can a batsman hit a cricket ball?

In the records section of the *Wisden Almanack*, the longest ever hit has for many years been attributed to an Oxford University student, Walter Fellows. *Wisden* states that in 1856, whilst at practice on the Christ Church ground in Oxford, Fellows drove a ball bowled by Charles Rogers 175 yards from hit to pitch.

Walter Fellows was a large man, apparently weighing over 17 stones at the time of his record strike. He was an aggressive middle order batsman who had a reputation for playing big shots: but even with the spring-handled and cane-handled bats that were in use by 1856, would it have been possible for the big-hitting Fellows to strike a ball 175 yards? Given that a six struck 100 yards is considered a long hit, it does not seem feasible for a ball to have been struck that distance.

The big hit was first reported in the *Oxford Chronicle and Berks and Bucks Gazette on* 26 April 1856. Under the headline 'A LONG HIT', the newspaper report read, 'During the last week, W Fellowes, Esq., of Christ Church, while engaged at cricket on the ground belonging to that Club, made one of the longest hits on record, the pitch of the ball being a distance of 175 yards.'

No mention was made in this brief article of the hit being at practice, or the name of the unfortunate bowler. Who wrote the brief newspaper report or supplied the story is not known, but the fact that Fellows' name is misspelt does not inspire confidence in its accuracy. It also states that this hit was only one of the longest, implying that there may have been longer ones!

No other cricketer has been credited with hitting a ball anywhere close to a distance of 175 yards. In 1899, Albert Trott famously hit a ball over the roof of the pavilion at Lord's, and remains the only player to have done so, but that has been estimated to be a distance of about 120 yards. The legendary Australian batsman Victor Trumper apparently struck a ball over 120 yards in a club match in 1903. In the modern era there have been some big hits claimed to be over 120 yards, but nothing approaching 175 yards.

So how did the *Wisden Almanack* find the story of the long hit, together with the additional information that was omitted from the original brief newspaper report? Perhaps by word of mouth. John Wisden, who started publishing his *Almanack* in 1864, the year after he retired from playing, was a leading allrounder from Sussex, who played for the England Elevens that travelled the country in the 1850s. A few months after his big hit Walter Fellows played at Lord's for an Oxford University team against the United All-England Eleven, which included John Wisden. There was to be no big hitting from Fellows in that match for Wisden dismissed him in both innings, for single figure scores, but Fellows might have told Wisden about his enormous hit.

Edward Martin was the head groundsman at Christ Church at the time and he was the person who 'carefully measured' the big hit. Martin's involvement immediately raises suspicions about the accuracy of the measurement because he was not just a groundsman, but also a cricket bat maker. Could it be that Fellows was using one of Martin's bats and that the bat maker suddenly saw a great marketing opportunity as he took out his tape measure? Edward Martin would also have known John Wisden, as they had played against each other a number of times, so perhaps it was Martin who provided the details which led to the story being included in the *Wisden Almanack*.

Of the three men known to be present at the time of the big hit, Edward Martin was the only one to have a possible financial benefit from the story, by promoting his cricket bats. Walter Fellows might have been happy to go along with the measurement that Martin provided in order to gain some notoriety. Professional Charlie Rogers would certainly not have been delighted to have been named as the bowler!

The following season Walter Fellows was one of 20 players who took part in a special match in Oxford, to trial a new version of a cane-handled bat that was being sold by Edward Martin: but whatever new bats have been designed over the years, no one has ever been able to come anywhere near to Fellows' reported record strike. The distance of 175 yards is unbelievable and the fact that it was Martin who measured it makes it very dubious. It is strange that the various editors of the *Wisden Almanack* never questioned it and the record hit continued to be included it in its annual editions over the decades.

As a footnote, there was another record set on the old Christ Church cricket ground in April 1859, when at the college sports day, Mr P Williams threw the cricket ball 109 yards, which was reported as the 'longest throw ever recorded by a member of the University'. Is it unkind to wonder whether this throw was also measured by Edward Martin?

The record did not last long as at the Exeter College sports day on Bullingdon Green in December 1859, Mr H Gillett threw a cricket ball the 'amazing distance' of 116 yards six inches. It was claimed that this distance had only ever been bettered by George Parr, the leading English batsman.

Edward Martin and his elastic tape measure were nowhere to be seen when this record was set!

Professionals Arrive – Rogers and Perry head North

The building of the railways provided a significant opportunity for professional cricketers in England. Previously, due to the difficulty of travelling any great distance, professional cricketers had to make a living from playing mostly in their own locality, although a small number were taken on by the Marylebone Club in London from the 1820s onwards. The railways provided an opportunity to travel long distances at speed and this made it much easier for Oxford colleges to recruit good professionals from around the country and not just rely on local talent.

One of the first outsider professionals to be hired at the University was John Brown, a Nottingham bowler, who was taken on by Wadham College to coach and be a practice bowler at their new ground to the north of the city in 1844.

By the 1850s, many colleges were hiring professional cricketers to be practice bowlers, coach the students, work on their grounds and sometimes play for them. They would come to Oxford in the early part of the season, before going off playing elsewhere from late June onwards. Many of these professionals that were employed at the University were of a high quality. In 1857, for example, amongst those hired by Christ Church were two fine Surrey and All-England players, Billy Caffyn and Tom Lockyer.

Surrey was one of the wealthier county clubs in the 1860s and paid their professionals handsomely: £3 a match, together with a win bonus of £1. The problem was that there were not many county clubs in existence and so the paucity of matches meant there was no great income to be earnt by professionals from just playing county cricket. Working at Oxford University was a good way of providing additional earnings.

In the 1860s an agricultural labourer could earn about 11s a week. By comparison, cricket professionals at colleges had the potential to earn perhaps five times as much. By 1862, Christ Church was paying 24s a week to practice bowlers, who were allowed to charge 1s 6d an hour for individual coaching sessions with students and were paid 7s 6d to play in a match, when they would also get a free dinner and a quart of beer. Professionals could also earn additional money through tips and wagers. In practice, Caffyn would sometimes persuade students to place a shilling on their stumps, which he would win if he bowled them.

There were also benefit matches for the professionals. In 1854, an admission charge of 1s was made for a two-day game between the University and the professionals at their grounds, with all of the proceeds going to the 'Players'.

Billy Caffyn earned his match fee and must have enjoyed his free quart of beer after scoring a chanceless 167 when playing for the Christ Church second team (assisted by three professionals) against the first team in May 1857. The *Oxford Journal* commented that it believed this to be the highest score ever made in Oxford, against 'fair bowling and fielding'. Looking back, it is hardly surprising that an All-England player could fill his boots when batting against students. Under the care of Edward Martin and through his use of his heavy rollers, the Christ Church ground was clearly a good pitch to bat on.

Despite the influx of cricketers, the best local professionals were also employed by colleges in the 1850s. David Burrin was one of these, working at various times at Oriel College, Christ Church and Balliol College. Another was Charlie Rogers, who was employed at Christ Church and Balliol College. Like Burrin, Rogers was a roundarm bowler, and they would often play together in the annual Town v Gown match in the 1850s. Their bowling in the 1854 fixture was described as 'first-rate', with Rogers taking seven wickets as the University was all out for 103.

Charlie Rogers was an enterprising Cowley professional, who was prepared to travel long distances to earn a living from cricket. For a few seasons in the mid 1850s, after the college season had finished, he went up to be the professional for a team at Eyton, in Shropshire. This led to him playing for Shropshire and Herefordshire sides whilst there. He had an impressive game for Shropshire against the All-England Eleven in 1857 and in later years played as a guest professional for various clubs against England teams.

Rogers went up to the north-west in 1858. There was no Lancashire CCC at this time, but he played professionally for Manchester CC, for whom he made his debut in first-class cricket in a match against Sussex.

In 1861 Rogers had a season as a professional at Lord's. One unusual match in which he appeared whilst there was for the Opposition v Government. Playing as a guest for the Opposition, Charlie claimed 12 wickets in the match, as the Government was defeated.

The following season Rogers journeyed to Scotland to be the professional at Kelso, whilst in 1863 he earned his money playing in Devon. Despite all of these forays around Britain, Charlie never moved permanently away from Cowley. He often worked locally as a labourer in the winter and went on to spend about 30 years as the professional/ groundsman at Balliol College.

William Perry was another Cowley cricketer, seven years younger than Charlie Rogers. He was a bowling allrounder who had caught the eye playing for Cowley as a youngster, being still only 16 when he was selected for the Bullingdon Union team to play against Berkshire in 1847. He must have impressed the opposition, as he was recruited to play a couple of matches for Berkshire in 1849, against local rivals Buckinghamshire.

Perry was a regular in the Cowley team and played in its important matches, such as the annual fixture against the

University. He was also selected by Edward Martin for the Oxfordshire sides that played the big games against Kent in 1849 and the All-England Eleven in 1850. That year, Perry joined David Burrin as a professional at the Reading club for the second half of the season.

Perry then headed north and began playing for the Liverpool club as a professional in 1854, with some success. He turned out for Liverpool and other clubs in the north-west against the travelling All-England sides and was then selected to play a few matches for both of the All-England teams, lining up with some of the biggest names in cricket. He played a first-class game for North v South in 1856 and found time to travel back home for the matches that the new Oxfordshire CCC had against Surrey in 1856 and 1857.

Perry remained the professional/groundsman at Liverpool throughout the 1860s. When the Lancashire County Cricket Club was founded, he was selected for its first ever county game, against Middlesex, in 1865. The Cowley lad had clearly become a Lancastrian by then!

As well as still playing, Perry also umpired some important games in and around Liverpool up until 1869, involving such teams as Lancashire and All-England. William Perry had a long and successful career as a cricket professional in Liverpool, but moved back to Oxford when it was over. He had not become a Lancastrian after all!

Charlie Rogers 1823 - 1887

William Perry 1830 - 1913

William Bacon – 'The Oxford Pet'

Whilst some of the best cricketers from Cowley were making a living from being professionals, a master batsman from Oxford, William Bacon, chose to play as an amateur. Later in life, however, Bacon was able to trade off his reputation and earned a living from selling cricket equipment for well over forty years.

William Bacon was born about 1814, near to the centre of Oxford. He was a genial, modest man, who worked as a servant at Brasenose College and lived on the Cowley Road, not far from Magdalen Bridge. Bacon became well known for his heavy run scoring at Cowley Marsh and he can be considered as the best batsman to come from Oxford in the 19th century.

Bacon played for the Oxford City club in the 1830s, which had become prominent after being founded by members of a reading and debating society in 1832. He became the leading batsman in the county in the 1840s, earning the nickname the 'Oxford Pet' (Oxford favourite). Bacon was a dependable opening batsman and his services were very much in demand. Apart from Oxford City, he would play for Cowley in their big matches, as well as a guest for many other teams. At a lower level he also played for the Brasenose Servants side, the Oxford Union team (which later changed its name to the United College Servants) and Long Vacation CC.

He played a lot of cricket and was obviously able to negotiate time off from his job at the University. A match that he played for Cowley against the University in 1843 was scheduled for three days, but because of bad weather was extended to five. Bacon top-scored for Cowley in both innings, so his employer might have rued the decision to give him extra time off.

William Bacon was a consistent run-scorer, and his best

season was 1849, when he came third in the national batting averages that had been compiled by the *Bell's Life* newspaper. In the 1840s, in the days before the *Wisden Almanack, Bell's Life* would collate all of the scores in 'first-rate' matches around the country and then publish the averages at the end of the season. In 1849, William Bacon scored 645 runs in top-class matches, with a highest score of 67, at an average of 23, which by present standards seems very low. Cricket pitches at the time were largely of a poor standard and even if a batsman could avoid being bowled by a low-bouncing shooter, the long grass on the outfield hindered heavy run-scoring. Bacon's average of 23 that year led to claims that he was one of the best batsmen of the day!

When the Bullingdon Union played a couple of matches against Berkshire in 1847, Bacon was one of the first to be chosen. Similarly, he played for the 16 of Oxfordshire against Kent in 1849. One of his finest hours came in the 18 of Oxfordshire v All-England match in 1850, when he scored 53 in a 'masterly manner' against some of the best bowlers in the country, before being run out.

In 1851, Bacon and Richard Hurst were the only local non-University players selected in the Oxfordshire 16 that took on the All-England Eleven. At the time, these two were described as 'two players of much celebrity in the locality'.

Although there was no Oxfordshire club during this period, rather surprisingly, Bacon also played a match for Berkshire in 1849, top scoring with 33 as his side was bowled out for 99 by Buckinghamshire.

Bacon took part in a number of single wicket matches and these games would often be played for money, despite the fact that he was an amateur cricketer. In 1849, Bacon had a match for £10 against Mr Aston from the University. The newspaper report stated that the 'Oxford Pet' won this game between 'two gentlemen of known cricket celebrity in the University and the city of Oxford'.

The following year there was a single wicket game on Cowley Marsh between William Bacon and two members of his family, against three Marsham brothers, who were sons of the Warden of Merton College. The brothers were talented cricketers, the eldest later playing for the Gentlemen of England, and they all bowled brisk roundarm. By contrast, the three Bacons all bowled slow underarm, but it was good enough, as they won the match, scoring 40 runs to the Marshams' 26. Single wicket games could be slow drawn-out affairs. This match lasted five hours!

In 1853, when only 39 years old, Bacon suffered a serious illness and had to give up his job as a college servant. Due to his popularity, a benefit fund was set up to support him and his family of six children.

As part of the fundraising for William Bacon, there was a two-day benefit match between an Oxfordshire team and Oxford City. Betting was still prevalent in cricket at this time and the first part of the match report in the *Oxford University Herald* described the fluctuating odds during the game. The betting appeared to be of as much interest to the newspaper reporter as the cricket match itself.

Before the match, the Oxfordshire team was the clear favourite, with its odds quoted at five to one on. On the second day of the game, when the Oxford club was set 65 to win, the betting was then evens. Those who had backed the county would have been celebrating when City collapsed to 12 all out in their second innings, with two Marsham brothers taking all ten wickets. Unfortunately for William Bacon, the match was thinly attended, due in part to the Reading Races falling on the same days.

There were a lot of donations to Bacon's benefit fund, and he used the proceeds to open a small tobacconist and cricket equipment shop in Broad Street, in the heart of the city. The shop was a success and he even managed to sell some cricket kit to the army during the Crimean War. It was reported in April 1855 that, 'Mr William Bacon, the well-known Oxford cricketer, last week forwarded to the Crimea a large assortment of cricket bats, balls, wickets, etc, to the order of Captain Dewar.'

Although no longer able to play to his previous high standard because of his poor health, William Bacon still appeared for the Oxfordshire team in the annual match against the University in 1854 and 1855. In August 1854, he also selected his own Oxfordshire side to take on a Berkshire team picked by Mr J Bowles of Milton Hill. William Bacon selected a good side, as Berkshire just hung on to draw the match. When an Oxfordshire CCC was finally set up in 1856, Bacon played one match for the county against Surrey, but failed to score in either of his innings. By then, his days as a leading batsman were over.

Bacon was a good organiser, and he clearly liked a bit of fun. In January 1856, when it was very cold, with Port Meadow freezing over, Bacon and Mr T Turner from the Oxford Unity CC, got a couple of teams together and played a cricket match on the ice!

William Bacon came from a large family and in 1867, he organised a match between a team of his extended family, all with the surname Bacon, against a College Servants side, on the Christ Church ground. Although he was now well over 50 years old and not in the best of health, William played in his side of Bacons, which included some of his brothers, sons and nephews. A large crowd attended and saw the eleven Bacons get the better of the College Servants. The fixture was played again in 1868, in front of an even larger crowd, and it seems a good day was had by all, with a band and dancing in the evening.

Bacon became President of Oxford City in the 1870s, which in the class-conscious Victorian era, was notable for someone who had been a humble college servant. This illustrated how well he was respected as both a cricketer and a person. He was a long-time advocate of setting up a county club and he served on the committee when a new

Oxfordshire CCC was eventually established in 1891.

Bacon was still running his shop, with one of his sons as an assistant, when he was in his late seventies, but he continued to suffer from poor health and died towards the end of 1899.

William Bacon was a very good batsman and an equally good man. As the *Oxford Chronicle and Reading Gazette* had commented at the time of his illness in 1853, 'He has long been as conspicuous for his skill in cricket as for his personal worth, intelligence and unassuming manners.'

A good man, who clearly deserved his nickname of the 'Oxford Pet'.

William Bacon 1814 - 1899

Bat and Ball makers – Pether and Harse

As cricket became more popular in Oxford, two enterprising families from the east of the city recognised the local need for bats and balls, and set about producing them. A father and son from the Pether family made bats in Cowley for more than 70 years, whilst many members of the Harse family manufactured cricket balls in Oxford over a period of 80 years.

Edward Martin had begun producing cricket bats in Oxford during the 1850s, but John Pether was making them in Cowley before then. Pether had trained as a carpenter, but with a lot of cricket being played on Cowley Marsh, branched out into bat making. His son Herbert Richard 'Dick' Pether joined his father as a 15-year-old apprentice and took over the business in 1876, which he advertised by placing a giant bat that was more than twice his height in front of his premises at 94 Cowley Road.

Dick played for Cowley CC in the 1880s, but it was for his skills as a maker and repairer of cricket bats that he became well-known. His cricket bats went on to be used by some of the leading batsmen in the country, such as England captains CB Fry and Pelham 'Plum' Warner, who had both started using Pether bats when students at Oxford University. Dick worked up until his death in 1911, when his business closed, as none of his apprentices wanted to take it on.

Dick Pether believed that the secret to bat making was to use the finest willow. There was a local supply of wood for the bat makers of Oxford, growing on the banks of the River Cherwell. Part of the grounds of Magdalen College is called Bat Willow Meadow and for many years the wood from the willow trees growing there has been used to make cricket bats.

A new cricket ball is a thing of beauty, but like anything of quality, a lot of skilled work is needed to make one. Before mechanisation made life easier, cricket balls were entirely hand-made and it needed expert craftsmen to create a ball of the correct weight and shape, with perfect stitching.

Dick Pether and his giant bat.

In the 18th century, Kent became the main area of cricket ball manufacture in England. When cricket balls began to be made in Oxford is not known, but as far back as 1776, there was a cricket ball maker working near the city centre. Come the middle of the 19th century, as college cricket and local club cricket began to flourish, a number of small firms of cricket ball makers sprung up in Oxford. The Harse family became the leading manufacturer in the area. Benjamin Harse, the son of a shoemaker, was the first of the family to venture into cricket ball making. He became an apprentice with John Best, who had been a ball maker on the Cowley

Road since the 1850s. Best was not an easy man to work with: in 1862, he even sacked his half-brother Edward Cooke, after a falling out. Cooke was an experienced ball maker, having left the Dukes firm in Kent a couple of years earlier in order to work for Best.

Best also had trouble retaining his apprentices and as soon as Benjamin Harse had learnt the skills of ball making, he left Best and set up his own cricket ball making firm just off the Cowley Road in 1871. Ben prospered, gaining a reputation for the quality of the balls that he made, selling them not just locally, but all around the country. He later took three of his younger brothers, Colin, Walter and Morton, into the business, as it grew.

In the census year of 1881, there were about 20 men living in Oxford and Cowley who were cricket ball makers. There were enough cricketers amongst them to set up their own team, the appropriately named Cricket Ball Makers CC, which played matches at Cowley Marsh. A trade union was even set up for the cricket ball makers of Oxford in 1891 and the new Amalgamated Society of Cricket Ball Makers was given a place in the Oxford Trades Council.

At this time there were about five Oxford firms making cricket balls. By then Colin, Walter and Morton had left their brother to set up their own cricket ball business, named Harse brothers. They later diversified into selling bicycles and illegal bookmaking, which proved more profitable than making cricket balls.

After the First World War, another younger brother, George Harse, set up a cricket ball making business just off the Cowley Road, with his son Harold. This continued up until the end of the 1930s. After the end of the Second World War, with George having died, Harold and his brother Norman set up a new Harse Brothers company, making cricket balls in St Aldates. Although there was a healthy demand for cricket balls from colleges and clubs, cheaper imported Indian balls soon proved stiff competition and the business closed in 1951. That proved to be the end of the Harse family involvement in cricket ball manufacture in the city and the production of their well-known 'Oxford' ball.

Robert Levens was an Oxford student in the 1920s and lodged with Harold Harse at his house in Divinity Road. He recalled that the Harse family were 'splendid company', who liked to socialise, but they were not well spoken and had a tendency to drop their Hs.

Somewhat unfortunate if your surname was Harse!

A Succession of Kings

The King family from Temple Cowley became well known in local cricket, not for what they could do with a bat or ball, but for the high quality of the cricket grounds under their care.

Sam King was at the head of the dynasty. He was born in 1840 and like his father and many of his brothers, worked as an agricultural labourer. His father played cricket for the Cowley team, as well in some single wicket matches at Cowley Marsh. Sam also went on to play for, and captain, the Cowley club, but it was as a groundsman that he excelled.

Sam King began working for the University on their cricket pitches at Cowley Marsh and in 1879 he was appointed as groundsman at the Magdalen Ground, at a salary of £40 per annum.

After many years of drawn-out discussions and wrangling, Oxford University Cricket Club finally acquired a new ground in 1881. Set in a beautiful location in the University Parks, close to the city centre, this ground was just what the University team needed (apart from the fact that part of the outfield sloped away). Impressed with his work at Cowley Marsh, the University appointed Sam King as the groundsman at the Parks, a position that he was to hold until 1918, by which time he was 78 years old. Sam did a very good job at the Parks and this was reflected by increases in his salary, which had doubled to £80 by 1887. By 1903 he was also being paid £43 by the University hockey club for maintaining their pitches in the Parks.

Sam was an early exponent of applying a loam dressing to cricket pitches and he earned a reputation for the quality of his work. 'He brought the care of grounds to a fine art,' wrote the *Oxford Chronicle*.

If Sam's 40 years of service as the University cricket

groundsman was impressive, then his four sons did even better. Edmund was the groundsman at the Brasenose College ground for 65 years, until reluctantly retiring at the age of 86. Sam's three other sons also had long careers as groundsmen at Oxford colleges: Herbert King worked at Balliol for 46 years, Percy King for 44 years at New College and Sam King junior 44 years at Merton.

Some of Sam's nephews also became cricket groundsmen. One of them, George 'Polly' King, was groundsman at University College from 1899 to 1935, a job he initially combined with being the landlord of the Original Swan pub in Temple Cowley. Another nephew William 'Fidler' King was the groundsman at Oriel College in the 1890s, as well as the landlord of the University Arms on the Cowley Road. (His nickname Fidler was apparently because he was untrustworthy, rather than any prowess on the violin.) Another more distant relative, William King, became a college groundsman after being the landlord of the Prince of Wales pub on the Cowley Road. Cricket and beer seemed to have a close connection in the King family. At their peak, it was reckoned that there were ten members of the King family working as college groundsmen.

At the end of the 19th century, the Cowley cricket club was the strongest in the county and many of the King family played in the team. Percy and Herbert King were prominent members of the side and when Cowley played in the County Cup final in 1899, there were four Kings in the team.

Because of his expertise, Sam was often employed to lay down the cricket square when new grounds were being created. Sam and his sons would travel as far as Devon to work on new grounds. Closer to home, in 1892, Sam laid out the cricket square at the new Abingdon ground on the Culham Road.

In 1899, the Littlemore club employed Sam King to lay out a wicket on their new ground in the village, and the following season there was an unusual match when Littlemore played

Sam King and his four sons.

against a Kings' Eleven. Sounding like a prototype of the Indian Premier League, a side was chosen by Sam King in which all eleven players had the surname King. Sam had a brother, four sons, three nephews and two grandsons in his team, as well as another grandson as 12th man.

The Kings' XI.

Alas, the Kings were defeated, being bowled out for 51, chasing Littlemore's meagre total of 59. Runs had been hard to score, as the wicket had been over-watered by the village groundsman. Surely not a mistake that the respected Varsity groundsman Sam King, or any of his descendants, would have made!

Sam King set a high standard with the cricket pitches that he prepared, but it seems that he was not the stereotypical 'grumpy' groundsman, for when he died in 1925, the *Sporting Life and Sportsman* wrote that Sam was 'a man of kindly and obliging disposition'. A lovely man who clearly loved his work.

Sam taught his sons well and just like their father, they were often praised for their work. In a review of the 1926 season, the *Oxford Times* highlighted the 'marvellous wickets' produced by Sam junior at the Merton College ground ... and the quality of the teas served by his wife Kate was also commended! Herbert would also boast that not a weed could be found on the outfield of his Balliol College ground and in the days before herbicides, he employed schoolboys to weed the field to ensure that was the case.

Edmund was Sam King's youngest son. After leaving school at the age of 12, he helped his father at the Parks, then worked on the grounds at Radley College, before becoming the groundsman at the new Brasenose College cricket ground in 1895, a job he held until 1959.

Edmund moved into the new groundsman's house on the Abingdon Road in 1903, where he lived for the rest of his life. He coached cricket and tennis and was a very active man. When the River Thames froze over in 1895, he skated down to Goring and back. Unfortunately, after an infection, he had a leg amputated in 1917 and had a wooden leg fitted, but this did not hold him back.

Edmund involved his family with the work at the Brasenose ground. His wife Annie not only did the catering but also helped her husband weed the outfield by hand. An old photograph also shows her guiding a horse which was pulling a mower around the outfield. Granddaughter Christine also remembered Edmund paying her a halfpenny for every plantain that she pulled out of the cricket pitch.

Over the years, Edmund became an institution at Brasenose College. When the Duke of Edinburgh visited the University in 1955, he was introduced to Edmund, who told him, 'I'm someone that you will never be. I am a King!' The college bursar promptly ushered Edmund away after that comment.

The Duke of Edinburgh meets Edmund King (right) when visiting Oxford in 1955.

Edmund was very industrious and also worked as the groundsman at the White House football ground, just over the road from where he lived. Like his brothers, he would sell cricket equipment to students and when they left it behind, would resell it. He also renovated bicycles and sold them to students. Edmund would also make money by organising 'entertainments' at the cricket pavilion and he helped set up the South Oxford Bowling Club and a new South Oxford Cricket Club at the Brasenose ground. He was never short of money and over time bought four houses in Marlborough Road, which he let out.

The King family made one major mistake as regards the family finances. In their younger days, Edmund and his brother Sam were friends of Billy Morris, as they all had an interest in cycling. Billy Morris got to know one of their sisters very well, but the family refused to let her marry Billy, as he was considered to be 'not good enough for our girl'. A quarter of a century later, thanks to his successful motor car company, William Morris was a multi-millionaire!

Two of Edmund's sons, Les and Monty, also became college groundsmen, although Monty had various groundsman's jobs around the country, including one at Aston Villa FC, before moving back to Oxford. Edmund's other son, Colin, went back to the family's roots, as he was the head teacher at Temple Cowley School from 1947 to 1963.

Sam King and his four sons were the exception in terms of being prosperous groundsmen. For the most part, you did not become wealthy being a college groundsman, but at least it was relatively secure and there was scope to have other part time jobs. When John Ambler was taken on as 'keeper' of the new Christ Church ground on the Iffley Road, in 1862, he was paid 18s a week, for which he had to superintend the boys, men and bowlers employed on the ground and also act as an umpire or bowler himself when required. A groundsman had the expense of providing his own horse to work on the ground, but tips would increase his earnings and a groundsman's wife usually made some money from catering. Many groundsmen also sold beer after a game, but when John Ambler applied for a licence to sell spirits in 1864, it was refused.

Pay rates did not improve much, for when David Burrin (nephew of the fast roundarm bowler of the same name) became the groundsman at Christ Church in 1892, he was paid £52 a year. He was still being paid the same in 1903, but by then he had probably doubled his earnings by also becoming the groundsman (and official starter) at the adjoining University Running Ground.

David Burrin, nephew of roundarm bowler, David Burrin.
Played for Cowley and Oxfordshire and was groundsman at Christ Church.

Being a college groundsman was a vocation for many, preferable to working in a factory, although not as lucrative. When Edmund King retired from his job as the Brasenose College groundsman, he was replaced by Norman Cofield and between them they served in the job for over 100 years. Clearly a lot of job satisfaction there.

Ray King was another long serving groundsman. Going back some generations, Ray was from the extended King family of Temple Cowley. He worked at the Southern By-Pass Ground before becoming the groundsman at St John's College in 1955, where he stayed until 1991. In Ray's era and before, being a college groundsman was often a job for your whole working life. Prior to Ray, Peter and Basil Rogers had between them worked on the St John's College ground since 1900, where North Oxford CC had begun playing in 1902.

Apart from the Kings, the Cowley families of Hodgkins,

Rogers and Burrin also produced generations of college groundsmen. David Hodgkins was a long-time groundsman at the Magdalen Ground, where he started working in 1831.

Another member of the family, William Hodgkins, worked as a bricklayer as well as being a groundsman on Bullingdon Green in the 1860s. William may have been a good groundsman, but he was not a good accountant. He was paid £30 a year by the Bullingdon Club to maintain their cricket ground and an additional £12 to collect the subscriptions and fees from the players. Something went awry in 1865 as he was prosecuted for embezzlement of monies belonging to the Bullingdon Club, but thankfully, was found not guilty.

Around this time, Billy Swain spent ten seasons as the professional and working on the cricket ground at Christ Church. The groundsman's skills learnt in Oxford proved very useful to Billy. Having emigrated to Australia in 1884, he became the first groundsman at the Gabba in Brisbane, when that cricket ground opened in 1895.

Heyday for the College Professionals

Come the start of the 1880s, college cricket at Oxford University was thriving. Most of it was still being played at Cowley Marsh, where there were 15 college grounds: a dozen, each with a wooden pavilion, on the Second Marsh (adjacent to Temple Cowley) as well as another three, including the Magdalen Ground, on the First Marsh (adjacent to the Cowley Road between what is now Howard Street and Magdalen Road). After the University team moved its home to the Parks in 1881, rather appropriately, Magdalen College began playing at the Magdalen Ground.

Most colleges played more than 20 matches in the short summer term, the vast majority amongst themselves, although there were a few games against schools such as Radley College and the odd one against local clubs.

With a lot of college cricket being played, there were plenty of job opportunities for cricket professionals. Around this time there were about 25 professionals working as coaches/ practice bowlers at college grounds, all of which also needed groundsmen, caterers, ball boys, etc. This was the heyday for professionals at the University, as the imminent development of the County Championship, which could provide season-long employment, would soon make it impractical for first-class county players to come to Oxford.

1884 saw Oxford University claim an historic victory over the touring Australians. It was a famous win, because it never happened again. Played at the Christ Church ground, because the University would not allow gate money be taken in the Parks, a crowd of over 4,000 came along on the third day to see the University score the winning runs. The 1884 Australian team had funded the cost of the tour themselves and had a keen interest in the size of the crowd, as it had agreed with the University club that it would receive half of the gate money. In the event, the total gate money taken for this match was a handsome £713. The large earnings of the Australians on this tour caused resentment amongst some of the relatively lowly paid English professionals that played against them.

The Professional Women Cricketers

By the 1880s a lot of cricket was being played in and around Oxford by men at all levels of society, but by very few women.

In 1884, Oxford University not only beat the Australians, but also, most importantly, Cambridge University. The Varsity match at Lord's had become a great annual social occasion by this time and in the report of the second day's play, the *Oxford Times* effused:

> The parade (at lunchtime) across the ground was as animated and as pleasing a spectacle as we remember to have seen ... Those who did not know how fair a thing is an English maiden in gala dress had ample opportunity on Tuesday to increase their stock of knowledge. It would be difficult to find at any gathering throughout the London season, a picture at once so varied, so full of life, and yet so thoroughly expressive of well-bred ease and luxurious idleness, as that presented by Lord's Cricket Ground on a great day.

In 1884, the idea that women would one day be playing at Lord's, rather than just parading across the outfield, displaying 'well-bred idleness', would have been shocking to the members of MCC.

In the 1880s, it was predominantly the upper classes that were playing women's cricket in England, either at country houses or at the small number of the women's clubs that had been formed. Sometimes there would be mixed games at country houses. At Nuneham Park, just to the south of Oxford, there was a match in August 1884 between 15 Ladies and 11 Gentlemen. Details of this match are limited, but it was reported that the Ladies won by five runs. Such games were probably more social than sporting occasions.

There was very little women's cricket being played in Oxford at this time. In 1885, there was a newspaper report stating that 'A ladies cricket club has been formed in Oxford and has acquired the permission of the University to play in the Parks.' This was probably a university team, although there were only a small number of female students at this point. In 1889, an 'Oxfordshire' women's team played against 'Hampshire' and the following year another 'Oxfordshire' side took on 'Gloucestershire' but these were one-off, unofficial county sides, made up of unrepresentative country house players.

In 1890, a private company called the English Cricket and Athletic Association Ltd established a squad of 30 professional women cricketers, with the stated aim of playing matches around the country to promote cricket as a suitable 'pastime for the fair sex in preference to Lawn Tennis and other scientific games'. Although its stated aim was to promote women's cricket, it was basically a money-making exercise. Nevertheless, it was a great innovation for its time.

In May of the following season, these 'Original English Lady Cricketers', as they were called, came to play in Oxford. An advertisement promoting their game stated that the cricketers would be 'elegantly attired', but also included a note that a matron would accompany the players, in order to ensure that things were kept 'select and refined'.

The English Lady Cricketers played a match between themselves, with the two teams unexcitedly named Reds and Blues. The organisers had special blue-coloured cricket balls made and presumably the Reds team bowled with a red ball, whilst the Blues used one of the new blue balls.

The game took place at the Old White House ground and despite an admission charge of 1s, a large crowd of about two thousand came to watch. The players were well paid, up to 35s a week, so the crowds at their matches needed to be sizeable in order to make the project worthwhile.

The Original English Lady Cricketers venture lasted only

a couple of seasons. Many women's clubs refused to play them, largely because it was seen as unbecoming for young ladies to be paid to play cricket.

Other travelling women's teams briefly sprung up, one of which was a side that came on the train from Windsor to play a mid-week game against the Abingdon men's club in 1892, but unfortunately this was a mismatch.

Very slowly, more women's cricket began to be played in and around Oxford. In 1892, an Oxford City Ladies team played a women's side from the University, although both sides were captained by men.

Miss Kathleen Madden, an enterprising young woman from Shotover, set up a team which in 1896 played Headington Quarry Second Eleven on Shotover Hill, with Kathleen, her sister Cicely, brother Algernon and eight other men in her side. Both of the sisters were 'exceedingly nimble with both bat and ball', according to a report in *Jackson's Oxford Journal*. Miss Madden's side played for a number of seasons against male or mixed sex sides. Perhaps inspired by Miss Madden, other female or mixed sex teams started to appear. In 1901 for example, Miss Madden's Eleven played against the all-female Miss Edwards' Eleven at Great Haseley and Miss Herschell's Eleven from Littlemore.

In late Victorian times, apart perhaps from on Feast or Celebration Days in villages, when there might be a Married v Single women's match, cricket was not for working women, as they had little leisure time.

Professional women's cricket never gained a foothold in the late Victorian era and indeed it would take a very long time to do so. The first England women's Test match was not played until 1934, and throughout the 20th century all of the players were amateurs. One of these was Oxford-born Debbie Stock, a batter/off spin bowler who played for England in the 1990s and was a member of the 1993 World Cup winning squad.

It was only in 2014 that the ECB first introduced professional contracts for women, awarding them to the top 18 English players. As the popularity of the game has grown in recent times, that number of ECB women's central contracts had jumped to 80 by early 2023, as well as at least 20 additional regionally funded contracts. All of a sudden professional women's cricket has taken off, with the Hundred competition providing a significant boost and the creation of a new Women's Indian Premier League taking it to a higher level again.

The *Holding Up a Mirror to Cricket* report in 2023 could also prove to be a game changer for women's cricket. The report called for women to have more power, voice and influence in the game, whilst the huge pay disparity between male and female professionals also needs to be addressed.

If the professional women's game can grow and flourish, perhaps the next England cricketer to come from Oxford could be female.

'Brusher' and Peter – Big-hearted Bowlers

As previously noted, Charlie Rogers (1823-1887) was one of the first wave of professional cricketers who came out of Cowley around the 1840s. He had six sons who went on to make a living as cricket groundsmen, some of them combining working on the grounds with coaching and/or playing professionally.

These six sons were:

Charles William Rogers (1850-1893)
Listed as a professional cricketer in the 1881 census, but not much is known about him.

Richard 'Dick' Rogers (1852-1947)
Groundsman/coach at Bedford Modern School for 43 years, played for Bedfordshire and became a Minor Counties umpire. His eldest son Henry 'Jack', and another son Cyril, were both school groundsman in Bedford. Another son, Basil, played briefly for Glamorgan and then Oxfordshire, and became the groundsman at St John's College.

Henry 'Bob' Rogers (1855-1945)
Groundsman at Worcester College for 52 years. His son William was a groundsman at Christ Church, a younger son, Percival, was groundsman/coach at Radley College, whilst another son, Reginald, was groundsman at Hertford College.

Joseph 'Joe' Rogers (1858-1930)
Groundsman at Magdalen College for about 40 years. His only son Fred succeeded him as the Magdalen College groundsman, and his son Joe was a fast bowler for Oxfordshire and Gloucestershire.

Alfred 'Brusher' Rogers (1863-1938)
Professional cricketer/groundsman who played as a pro both locally and at Accrington. Had a distinguished

career for Oxfordshire and was the Exeter College groundsman for about 40 years. One of his sons, 'Len', was a club professional/groundsman for a brief period and played for Oxfordshire. Youngest son Neville became a professional for Hampshire, batting consistently well after the Second World War.

Peter Rogers (1866-1923)
Professional cricketer/groundsman. Also had a lengthy career for Oxfordshire and was groundsman at St John's College. His only son Bert played a few games for Hampshire before the First World War.

Quite a family! Of Charlie's sons, it was the two youngest, Alfred and Peter, who were the best cricketers. They were good bowlers.

Why Alfred was nicknamed 'Brusher' is not known, but what is clear is that he was a fiery fast bowler, not slow to exchange a few words with the opposition. Peter, a small man with a large moustache, bowled off cutters, with great skill. He was calmer than his brother and well thought of.

Peter captained the Cowley club for a period, as did Brusher after him, and under them, the club won many trophies. Both could also bat, although they usually came in lower down the order when playing for Oxfordshire, due to the large amount of bowling that was required of them. Matching his personality, Brusher was a hard-hitting attacking batsman, whilst Peter was capable of opening the batting.

Brusher was born in 1863 and Peter came along three years later. When he was only five years old, Brusher lost the sight in his left eye in an accident, but this did not hold him back. As boys, Peter and Brusher would sometimes skip school in order to earn money by collecting balls at college practice sessions on Cowley Marsh. Both began playing cricket for Cowley and they soon showed their ability.

As a 16-year-old, Brusher was taken on as a practice bowler at Worcester College in 1880 and he began playing for Oxford

City that year, making an instant impact by taking six first-innings wickets in a game against MCC. The following season his fast bowling for Oxford City was deadly, as he claimed 63 wickets at a cost of only eight runs apiece and he was selected for a one-off Oxfordshire match against Berkshire. By the time he celebrated his 18th birthday in August 1881, Brusher was well on the way to becoming a local legend!

Brusher ventured north to play as a professional for Accrington for two full seasons in 1883 and 1884, as well as the odd game in the following three years. The Lancashire pitches clearly suited his bowling, as in total he took 157 wickets in 46 games in the 1883 and 1884 seasons. Quoting statistics can get tedious, but there is no avoiding them in Brusher's case, as year after year his figures were outstanding.

When Brusher returned home, the brothers would play together for Cowley and could be devastating. In 1888, Peter and Brusher took all 20 wickets as Headington Quarry was bowled out for 37 and 35 in a game against Cowley. Older brother Joe Rogers also top scored with 30 in Cowley's total of 150.

Peter Rogers became the professional at Torquay in 1893, followed by a spell as groundsman/coach/professional bowler at the Military Staff College in Camberley. He came back permanently to Oxford in 1900, when he became the groundsman at the St John's College ground.

When a new Oxfordshire CCC was set up in 1891, Peter and Brusher were recruited as professional bowlers. Year in, year out, they bowled their hearts out for their county, rarely failing to take wickets.

Peter Rogers was the more successful of the brothers in the early years and when Oxfordshire entered a new Second Class County Championship in 1895, he was the leading wicket taker in the competition that season, with 60 victims in just eight matches. That year, the brothers took all 20 wickets, shared equally, in a game that Oxfordshire managed to lose to Buckinghamshire. In the following match Brusher took nine for six in Bedfordshire's first innings of 32 all out, whilst Peter claimed seven wickets in the match. When they were on song, the Rogers brothers called the tune.

When Oxfordshire had a fine victory over Berkshire in 1897, the brothers played a big part. Brusher scored a chanceless century (apparently the first ever made against Berkshire) and they took 14 wickets between them. Peter also took his best ever figures of nine for 20 against Berkshire in 1900. On their day the Rogers brothers could scythe through a batting line up ... and they had many good days!

Between them, they spent a lot of time on the cricket field. In 1899 as an example, as well as playing for his local Cowley club, where nobody was paid, Brusher earnt money by taking 53 wickets at an average of less than nine for City and 24 wickets at a cost of seven and a half runs each for Witney. On top of that, he took 35 wickets at an average of 20.7 for the county. At Oxford City, Brusher also earned some additional shillings by coaching club members and bowling at them in the nets. He must have been very resilient.

Come the turn of the century, Peter and Brusher continued to be the backbone of the county bowling attack. As the *Oxford Times* commented about Oxfordshire's 1901 season, 'The brothers Rogers have repeatedly come to the rescue,' when things were going badly. Brusher was given a benefit by the county that year, taking the meagre income from the wet county cricket week, but his popularity ensured that through collections and donations, he received £100 in all. Two years later, Oxfordshire CCC also gave Peter a benefit.

In September 1902, Peter and Brusher played for the City team that was bowled out for just 60 by Witney. Returning to play as a guest for his old club, Gilbert Jessop took nine Oxford City wickets (he was deprived of a chance of a tenth by the No 11 batsman being absent). A month earlier Jessop had become a national sporting hero by scoring a century off only 76 balls, as England defeated Australia by one wicket in the final Test at the Oval. Sporting hero or not, Jessop was dismissed by Brusher for 14 when he batted for Witney in this game.

For many seasons, Witney would employ Brusher and/ or Peter to play in their most important fixtures. The day after Jessop's devasting bowling, Peter and Brusher played for Witney against Hon R Hardinge's Eleven, when a crowd of over 1,000 turned up to see an aged WG Grace playing for Witney. In the first innings, WG and Brusher opened the bowling and between them they took all ten wickets, Brusher taking the lion's share of six. In the same fixture the following season, Peter played for Hardinge's side and dismissed Grace for 13.

Brusher became the captain of Cowley in 1904 and that year a newspaper wrote, 'Men may come and men may go, but Brusher goes on for ever. What would Oxfordshire, Cowley or City have done without him.' It commented that his staying power was remarkable, due to the fact that he was 'as strong as a horse' The fitness of the two brothers was outstanding, as they hardly ever missed a game through injury.

Come the 1906 season, Peter stopped playing for the county, but Brusher continued and despite losing some of his zip, on occasions 'bowled just as well as ever'. The county club folded at the end of 1906, by which time, between them, the brothers had taken 998 wickets for Oxfordshire in games against other counties between 1891 and 1906, 813 of them in the Minor Counties Championship. A magnificent performance!

So just how good a bowler was Brusher Rogers? Could he have held his own in first-class cricket? Hubert Bassett was a seam bowler who played first-class cricket for Oxford University for four seasons before becoming a regular in the

Oxfordshire team alongside the Rogers brothers. In first-class cricket, Bassett took 78 wickets at a healthy average of 22.1, but the wickets that he took for Oxfordshire came at a higher average and inferior strike rate to Brusher's. On that comparison, Brusher could have prospered in the first-class game, if he had been prepared to permanently move away from Temple Cowley.

Brusher played out his final cricketing years at Cowley. He continued as a college groundsman and worked on the University golf course at Cowley Marsh. (Both Peter and Brusher were also talented golfers: in a competition at Malvern in 1903, Brusher reportedly had a round of 74 in 'testing conditions'.) Brusher also did some coaching, such as at the Clarendon Press club, where he worked for three evenings a week in 1909. He played the odd game up until the outbreak of war, as well as doing some umpiring.

After the First World War, Brusher continued as the groundsman for the University golf club and also umpired. Peter carried on as the groundsman at St John's College and took pride in maintaining the cricket ground, tennis courts and bowling green to a high standard. He took up bowls, at which he soon became an expert.

Peter's health began to fail, but it was still a shock when he died in 1923, at the age of 57. As one of the speakers at the subsequent Oxford City annual dinner remarked, Peter Rogers had been 'the prince of Oxford cricket'. If Peter was the prince, then it would be fair to say that Brusher was the king.

Up for the Cup

In 1889, letters to the *Oxford Times* suggested that local cricket should take a lead from football and set up some cup competitions. The following year a new City Challenge Cup competition began, which was open to all clubs within a three-mile radius of Carfax, although the top clubs such as Oxford City and North Oxford were excluded and no professionals were allowed. This new competition proved popular and as Captain Airey had donated most of the money to purchase the trophy, it soon became known as the Airey Cup.

In 1894, a new County Cup was set up for the best clubs in Oxfordshire, which Witney won in the first year. Gilbert Jessop, who was then a 19-year-old trainee teacher at Burford Grammar School, had the incredible match bowling figures of 19 for 32 for Witney in the final against the Victoria club from Oxford.

Cowley soon came to dominate this County Cup: after losing in the 1895 final, Cowley won three years running after that, with Peter and Brusher Rogers leading from the front. In the 1896 final, Thame was bowled out for 20 and 24 as Cowley won on the first of two scheduled days. On a responsive wicket the Rogers brothers took all 20 wickets.

The following year, Cowley defeated Star in the final, with the Rogers duo claiming all of the wickets in the Star second innings, after Brusher had taken seven in the first. The same two teams played in the 1898 final, which was a three-day match. Cowley won again, by 270 runs, with Peter scoring a century and Brusher taking ten wickets in the match.

The Cowley dominance had a detrimental effect, as only six clubs entered the competition in 1899. In a remarkable sporting gesture, the Rogers brothers agreed not to play in the County Cup that year, in order to encourage the other clubs. In their absence, Star managed to beat Cowley in the final. The following year, the two Rogers were back in the Cowley team, which went on to win the cup again for the fourth time in five seasons, easily beating South Oxford in the final. Brusher took 11 wickets in the final and on occasions 'bowled as fast as he had ever done'. The Rogers brothers were simply too good!

By 1901, there was much debate about what was to be done about the Cowley domination of the faltering County Cup. The Chairman of the organising committee bemoaned the fact that there was not another county in England 'in which a little knot of professional cricketers resided in such a small radius and were able to form a club which would knock every other out'. The solution for the 1901 season was to exclude from the cup anyone who had played for the county team on three occasions or more the previous year. This meant that the two Rogers and also Fred Arnold could not play for Cowley and in their absence, South Oxford went on to win the cup.

With only a handful of teams taking part, the County Cup was changed into a league competition, but this did not stop Cowley winning it again in 1902 and 1903. The Rogers duo were again to the fore, with Brusher's bowling in the 1903 competition being decisive, as he took five for eight against Oxford City, seven for 24 against South Oxford and six for 35 against Littlemore.

Due to a lack of interest, the County Cup competition ceased in 1904, but clubs within Oxford were keen to set up a league. In 1905 the Oxford Cricket League began, with two divisions, in which there were five teams each. The grounds of competing clubs had to be within four miles of Carfax and all players needed to have a family home within that same distance. Cowley, Oxford City, North Oxford, South Oxford and the College Servants played in Division One.

Being the groundsman on their St John's College home

pitch, Peter decided to play for North Oxford in the new Oxford Cricket League. The Rogers brothers battled it out against each other in that first league season. When North Oxford easily beat Cowley at home, Peter opened the batting, scored 63 and took six wickets, including that of his brother. In the return match at Cowley, Brusher gained his revenge, taking seven for 31, which included snaring his brother lbw. Brusher's Cowley won the Oxford Cricket League in 1905, but Peter's North Oxford was victorious the following season.

By now Peter and Brusher were nearing the end of their playing days, but Peter carried on turning out for a few years more and was in the Cowley team that beat Cowley St John in the league final of 1911.

Alfred 'Brusher' Rogers 1863 - 1938
Minor Counties Championship 1895 - 1906 89 matches
488 wickets @ 15.7 & 1,928 runs @ 16.3

Peter Rogers 1866 - 1923
Minor Counties Championship 1895 - 1905 79 matches
325 wickets @ 17.4 & 1,470 runs @ 13.9

County cricket – Missing the Boat

For decades, teams calling themselves Oxfordshire had played matches, even going back as far as 1779, when there had been a county game against a Berkshire side at Henley-on-Thames. These were usually one-off matches between gentlemen cricketers.

It was not until the 1840s and again in the 1850s that an Oxfordshire County Cricket Club was established, but both of these were short-lived. The demise of these clubs represented missed opportunities, because due to the early development of cricket at the University, there was a strong group of local professionals in this era, including the Burrin brothers, Charlie Rogers and William Perry, as well as some good amateurs, such as William Bacon, the Hurst brothers, James Fletcher and the university-educated Marsham brothers. All that was needed to form a strong county club was some leadership, finance and land on which to build a ground. The Hurst brothers had land and money, but sadly there was no one who could provide the leadership necessary to sustain an Oxfordshire county club.

By the 1880s, whilst there was no Oxfordshire club, a number of other strong county clubs had been formed around the country and newspapers would print league tables to determine the champion county. It was all rather disorganised and it was not until 1890 that eight county clubs, namely Gloucestershire, Kent, Lancashire, Middlesex, Nottinghamshire, Surrey, Sussex and Yorkshire, played under agreed rules, in an organised County Championship.

Whilst first-class cricket developed, Oxfordshire was left behind. A major problem was the attitude of the men who were influential in Oxford cricket. They were old-school, upper-class amateurs who were content to play friendly, social cricket, on grounds rented from the colleges. They had no desire to form a county club to play competitive first-class cricket.

By the 1880s, the City club was grandly calling itself the Oxford City and County CC. At its annual dinner in 1884, the President, Lord Jersey, when considering the prospect of a possible new Oxfordshire club said, with some disdain, that 'No county club has a chance these days unless they have the assistance of professionals.' He hoped that the Oxford City and County club would not run away with the idea that the sole object of its existence was to play against Yorkshire, or some of the premier counties. He thought that they should always bear in mind that one of the great benefits of the club was to give everybody a chance of playing in a game!

With such an attitude from the men at the top, cricket in Oxford and Oxfordshire had no chance of progressing. Those lower down the social scale kept trying, however. At the same club dinner, the following year, William Bacon made a speech, asking for the local authority to help. 'If the Corporation could provide the club with a ground,' he said that he would 'do his best to find an eleven to meet any county.'

Eventually, after years of missed chances and apathy, a new Oxfordshire County Cricket Club was established in February 1891. Over the following four seasons Oxfordshire played friendly games against the University, other nearby counties and MCC. Unfortunately, injuries and problems of availability meant that the new county club could seldom field a strong side and results were not encouraging.

In 1895, the first-class County Championship was enlarged to 14 teams, but Oxfordshire was not one of them, as it entered a new Second Class County Championship instead.

Oxfordshire had a moderate record in the early years of the Second Class (soon to be known as the Minor Counties) competition. The Rogers brothers bowled well, but the Cowley wicketkeeper-batsman Fred Arnold, who played as the third professional in the county team, could seldom reproduce the batting form that he showed for Cowley.

Attempts were made to find a home ground for the county club, which it could have shared with Oxford City. In the mid 1890s, Mr George Morrell, of Headington Hill House, offered the lower part of South Parks, which was in his ownership, for the site of a ground. Unfortunately, the City Surveyor quashed this. Another idea was to build a ground on the highest section of Port Meadow, but this never materialised.

The availability of good quality college cricket grounds which both the county and Oxford City could use meant there was no pressing need to find a permanent ground. But the lack of its own ground was a drawback for the county, as it would have provided a home for the club with unlimited access and the potential to develop.

Come the early 1900s, the left-arm seamer Hubert Bassett and the Rogers duo continued to share the bowling load for Oxfordshire, but inconsistent batting let the team down.

The county captain, Charles Brownrigg, wrote a letter to the *Oxford Times* at the end of the 1902 season stating that 'Lack of funds and extraordinary lack of interest still hang as heavy millstones around the neck of Oxfordshire cricket.' Over the years, part of the reason for this lack of interest from players and spectators was that a lot of local cricketing talent tended to be ignored when county teams were selected. The young cricketers from Oxford who emerged at this time and went on to become professionals had little or no assistance in their development from their county club.

The county captains who picked the sides often had scant first-hand knowledge of cricket in Oxfordshire. Charles Bradford was skipper around the turn of the century, but he worked as a schoolmaster in Bristol. In 1904 Fred Marsh skippered the county, but he was away at Cambridge University for the first part of the season. His brother,

James, was also in the county team, but he was a clergyman who lived far away from Oxford. There was no local heart to the Oxfordshire team.

Player availability was also a problem. Apart from the professionals, most of the others in the county team were those who could either afford to take time off work or had jobs such as teachers and clergymen, where they had plenty of spare time to go off playing cricket in late July and August. There were often many university-educated players from the better off upper echelons of society in the Oxfordshire team, which was unrepresentative of the cricketers playing in Oxford and the county as a whole. Little wonder there was an 'extraordinary' lack of local interest in the county side.

1905 saw Oxfordshire finish bottom but one of the Minor Counties Championship. In a match at Reading, Berkshire was at one stage 370 for one in its first innings, before Brusher Rogers fought back to take five for 115, as Oxfordshire escaped with a draw. It was tough going, both on and off the pitch. Total gate money from home matches was only £6 in 1905, as the club ran up a deficit of £150.

By the start of the 1906 season fund-raising appeals had allayed the financial crisis and the county team managed to play on for another year. The *Oxford Times* commented that the county of Oxfordshire should be ashamed of the position in which the county club found itself: 'It has always been a standing disgrace to Oxfordshire that they have never been properly able to support a county club, either by the appeals to generosity of the public or through the aid of gates.' Come late 1906, with the bank owed £130 and requiring payment by the end of the year, Oxfordshire CCC was wound up.

So Oxfordshire had not only missed the boat in the period between the mid 1840s and mid 1890s, when it would have been possible to establish a top-class county club, but by 1906 the Oxfordshire ship had well and truly sunk. The implication of this for young cricketers from Oxford was that if they wanted to become professional first-class county cricketers, they would have to move away to another county. A major deterrent to this was the residential rule that existed at this time, whereby a cricketer had to live in a county for two years before being allowed to play for it in the County Championship.

There are similarities in how county cricket developed in Oxfordshire, compared with Cambridgeshire, its academic rival. University cricketers playing on common land were an early impetus to the game in both Oxford and Cambridge, leading to the locals taking up cricket and some becoming good enough to play professionally. By the 1850s, both Oxfordshire and Cambridgeshire had talented bands of professionals, but in both counties, a lack of finance and will meant that county clubs could not be sustained. In both Oxford and Cambridge, their universities provided employment opportunities for talented cricketers, but these powerful academic institutions were self-centred and insular, with no interest in promoting or supporting a county cricket club.

Some of the matches that Cambridgeshire sides played in the middle of the 19th century have been given first-class status, but that was the pinnacle for cricket in the county. Both Oxfordshire and Cambridgeshire went on to join the Minor Counties competition in the 1890s and with a few hiccups along the way, have never progressed any further.

City Boys – Leaving Home

It is ironic that whilst Oxfordshire CCC slid into oblivion in the early 1900s, there were a number of Oxford-born cricketers playing professionally elsewhere around the country. Five of these players had a connection with the Oxford City club. One of them was the deadly Surrey off-spinner William 'Razor' Smith and his story will be told later. The other four were:

HARRY HUGGINS

Harry Huggins was an Oxford man who played for the City club before becoming a professional with Gloucestershire, for whom he played from 1901 to 1921. Harry was a fast-medium bowler and in his early years, when conditions suited him, could take down a batting line-up. In 1902, Huggins took seven for 17 against Sussex at Hove, and then seven for 37 against Worcester later in the season. He bettered this in 1904, taking nine for 34 against Sussex at Bristol, bowling eight batsmen, with the other caught and bowled. Harry obviously bowled very straight.

Huggins had 11 steady seasons for Gloucestershire, but his performances tailed off in the years immediately before and after the First World War. Lack of fitness was the problem for Harry and according to *Wisden*, 'He put on weight ... and his brilliant days grew infrequent.'

After his playing career was over, Harry played club cricket for Stroud. He also acted as scorer for Gloucestershire for a while. Many ex-pros go into coaching, some become umpires, but scoring for your county, that is a rare one!

Harry Huggins 1877 - 1942
First-class 1901 - 1921 200 matches
584 wickets @ 29.0 & 4,375 runs @ 14.4

LEVI WRIGHT

Levi Wright was born and bred in Oxford, but having played cricket for Oxford City, moved to Derby to take up a teaching job. Levi impressed in local cricket, and he began playing for Derbyshire in 1883. He was a stylish batsman and fine fielder, his speed of foot leading him to play football for Derby County.

Wright was a late developer, not scoring his initial first-class century until the age of 35 and by the time that he was named as one of *Wisden's* Cricketers of the Year in 1905, he was 43 years old.

Levi played mostly as an amateur, but towards the end of his career gave up teaching and worked on the railways as a clerk in the winter, whilst playing for Derbyshire as a professional.

Levi Wright 1862 - 1953
First-class 1883 - 1909   325 matches
15,166 runs @ 26.1

JACK PARSONS

The son of a chef at Brasenose College, as a child Jack Parsons lived in the centre of Oxford and went to watch his father play cricket for Oxford City. In 1898, when Jack was only eight years old, the family moved to Coventry. Parsons showed early promise as a cricketer and went on to sign for Warwickshire as a professional in 1910, at a wage of £75 for the summer and £1 a week in the winter. Scoring well, he soon established himself in the side and received a £10 bonus and a watch when Warwickshire won the County Championship in 1911.

Parsons was a forceful, attacking batsman, never quite in the right place at the right time to gain selection for England. He had long break from cricket when serving in the army, winning the Military Cross for his bravery. He returned to play for Warwickshire, having spells as both a professional and an amateur.

Parsons became a clergyman and was not afraid to speak his mind. When he went on an MCC tour to India in 1926/27, as a professional, he was reportedly 'openly critical of social and racial discrimination' which he encountered on the trip. Professionals in those days were meant to keep their heads down and tow the line, but Jack was formidable both as a batsman and as a man.

Jack Parsons had a long and eventful life. He often came back to play charity matches in Oxford, but despite his long cricketing career, never played at the Parks, the ground that was only a few streets away from his boyhood home.

Jack Parsons 1890 - 1981
First-class 1910 - 1936 355 matches
17,969 runs @ 35.7 & 83 wickets @ 29.0

EDWIN WAKELIN
Despite the growth of county cricket by the early 1900s, there were still opportunities for cricketers to earn a living as club professionals. One such was the Oxford player Edwin Wakelin, who became a successful club professional in the Midlands and whilst there, also played a single match for Worcestershire.

Edwin Wakelin's family lived just off the Cowley Road, not far from Magdalen Bridge, and his father worked as a college servant. Young Edwin came to prominence at his local Cowley St John club and went on to play for Oxford City and Oxfordshire. He turned down an invitation to qualify for Essex in 1904 and took the job of professional at Bournville CC instead. Bournville, which was located just to the south of Birmingham, was the home of the Cadbury chocolate factory. Wakelin did well at Bournville and was employed by the club up until the First World War. Although he was a bowling allrounder, he scored over 2,000 runs in a season on more than one occasion.

As well as a factory, the Cadbury family built housing and extensive sporting facilities at Bournville, including a scenic cricket ground. Worcestershire played a couple of matches there in 1910 and in the first of these against Essex, they asked Edwin Wakelin to play for them. Rain ruined this match, but at least Edwin had a very brief taste of first-class cricket.

After the First World War, Wakelin returned to Oxford and played for Oxfordshire up until the season before his untimely death at the age of 44.

Edwin Wakelin 1880 - 1925
Minor Counties Championship 1902 - 1924 32 matches
85 wickets @ 18.8

'Razor' Smith's Match 1912

'Monday September 9th, 1912 will go down to posterity as a "red letter day" in the history of Oxford cricket. For the first time in living memory a first-class professional team came to play against an Oxfordshire side. The match was arranged with a two-fold object – firstly to assist the laudable cause of charity; secondly to stimulate interest in the game with a view to resuscitating the defunct Oxfordshire County Cricket Club.'

Oxford Times 14/9/1912

The Surrey bowler 'Razor' Smith, who was from Oxford, was given a benefit in 1912 and in conjunction with the *Oxford Times* brought a team of professional county players to the city for a charity match against an Oxfordshire Eleven on 9 September. Whilst the proceeds of this match went to charity, collections for Razor's benefit were held at local matches all around Oxford that season.

The Oxfordshire side for this game was selected in a most unusual way. Readers of the *Oxford Times* were asked to vote for the players they thought should be in the team and according to the newspaper an extraordinary number of votes were sent in. The Oxfordshire side that was duly formed put up a good fight, scoring 148, which Razor Smith's team chased down, but only with some difficulty. A crowd of more than 3,000 came to watch the match which proved a great success. Sadly, there was not enough lasting enthusiasm to bring about the founding of a new county club.

Razor's side included mostly Middlesex, Hampshire and Surrey players, one of whom, the former England batsman Tom Hayward, would take over as groundsman/coach in the Parks in 1918. Apart from Razor, there were three other professionals who had been born in Oxford in his team, namely the Hampshire pair of Alec Bowell and George Brown, together with Jack Parsons of Warwickshire.

'Razor', or William Charles Smith as he was christened, had been born in Oxford, back in 1878. He grew up in a working-class family that lived on the Cowley Road, with a father who was a former soldier and ran a beer house. Smith began playing cricket for the Boulter Street Working Men's Institute and then the Oxford City colts team. His talent must have been clear from a young age, because by 1895 he was playing as an allrounder in the Oxford City first team. Smith went on to be selected for a couple of Oxfordshire matches in August 1897, both of which finished in heavy defeats, as he failed to take a wicket. Somehow, he developed a connection with Surrey and in the same month was keen enough to travel up to Sunderland to play in a friendly for Surrey Second Eleven against Durham.

Smith moved to London and by 1900 was playing for WG Grace's London County side, but having impressed in a Surrey trial match, he was selected to make his County Championship debut against Derbyshire. He promptly took five wickets in the first innings, although he could not dislodge the Derbyshire opener, Levi Wright, who made a century.

Smith was given the nickname 'Razor' by a Surrey team-mate, Tom Richardson, because he was extremely thin. He had a frail body and was often injured which meant that he was in and out of the Surrey team over the next few seasons.

Smith bowled sharp off breaks and on a wet pitch could be almost unplayable. In 1904 when Surrey bowled out Hampshire for 71 at The Oval, Smith claimed nine for 31. On his day he could be deadly, but he could not keep fit enough to last a whole summer.

It was not until the 1909 season that Razor flourished. He took 12 of the 16 Australian wickets to fall when Surrey played the Aussies that year. If that was good, then the following season Razor was sensational, as he claimed a staggering 215 wickets for Surrey in the County Championship! Only two other bowlers have surpassed that total in the history of the competition. His finest match in 1910 came at The Oval against Northamptonshire, when he took six for 16 and then eight for 13, including a hat-trick, as the visitors were bowled out twice on the second day for the same score of 51. When Surrey travelled to Northampton in the return fixture later in the season Razor could not repeat his previous heroics ... as he only took 11 wickets in that game!

1911 was another good season for Razor, as only one other bowler in the country took more wickets than him and he was selected for Test Trials in 1911 and 1912. With doubts about his fitness, he was never picked for England and his weak body continued to let him down through to his final season in 1914. Despite the success that he had in his career, Razor could have been more prolific if only he could have stayed fit.

William 'Razor' Smith.

When healthy, Razor Smith could be unstoppable. As *The Cricketer* wrote in 1929, 'Smith was a great performer on his day and to those who remember his wonderful bowling in the pre-war period, he will always remain as one of the finest bowlers in the history of the game.'

'One of the finest' all-time bowlers is praise indeed, albeit over the top. However, Razor's record of taking five wickets in an innings on 95 occasions, when he only played 245 matches, illustrates his prowess. If only England had a spinner of his calibre today! If he was playing now, Razor would also have the benefit of a strength and conditioning coach, to keep him fit and healthy.

Razor was a lower order batsman of no great repute, but just occasionally he would prosper. He went on the MCC tour to the Caribbean in 1912/13 and whilst his bowling was not noteworthy, Razor did manage to score 126, when batting No 11, in a match against Barbados.

During his playing days, he began working in the winter for the bat maker Stuart Surridge, in the south of London, and after retiring from cricket, he continued to work there. Having discarded his bowling boots, Razor also coached at Cambridge University, as well as the Surrey and Essex nurseries. In the winter of 1929/30, he became the first English professional to go over to coach for the Ceylon Cricket Association.

When a Surrey player, Razor would often come back and play games for Oxford City in September, after the first-class season had ended. A popular player, he always received a good reception in his home city.

Razor Smith could certainly turn the ball sharply and must go down as the best spin bowler ever to have come from Oxford.

William 'Razor' Smith 1878 - 1946
First-class 1900 - 1914 245 matches
1,077 wickets @ 17.6

Elmer Cotton's Shop

A talented 29-year-old batsman joined the Oxford City club at the start of the 1910 season and made an immediate impression, scoring plenty of runs in his first few matches. Later in the summer he made an undefeated double-century against the touring South Kensington team and the *Oxford Times* commented that, 'He is a class above any batsman in this city.'

Elmer Cotton was this player. His distinctive name will be familiar to many local cricketers, because of the shop that he ran in Turl Street, in the heart of Oxford. When he took over the shop in 1910 it was a tobacconist, but under Elmer it began to sell sports equipment and became a small treasure trove for generations of cricketers. For cricket kit, Elmer Cotton's was the place to go.

Elmer Cotton had grown up in the south of London and was a promising young cricketer, playing for Surrey Second Eleven in the Minor Counties Championship in 1905 and 1906. Having moved to Oxford and scored well for City in his first season, he was elected club captain in 1911. He was also made captain of the Oxfordshire team that played Razor Smith's side in 1912 and scored an attacking half-century in that match, which impressed his professional opponents. The quality of Elmer's innings was noted by Razor Smith, who wrote, 'We all know him to be a first-rate bat, having played with him at The Oval on several occasions some years ago, but he surprised even us.'

Cotton was also a good amateur footballer and joined Oxford City FC at the start of the 1910/11 season, going on to be one of their most reliable and versatile players over the next few seasons. Whilst at Oxford City, Elmer was selected for some England AFA representative matches. In July 1914, Elmer combined his two main sports when he opened the batting for a team of Oxford City footballers in a cricket match against the Isthmian League.

With the outbreak of war, Elmer went off to serve in the army and then in the newly formed RAF, with his brother Bill taking over the running of the shop. Having survived the war, Cotton returned to play cricket for Oxford City. In 1921 he showed that he had not lost his touch, when scoring 187 for City in a league game against Cowley.

Elmer played for the new Oxfordshire CCC when it was set up in 1922, although he was in his early 40s by then. In 1925 he was made county captain and he continued playing off and on for Oxfordshire up until 1931. Being past his best, he never scored heavily for Oxfordshire, but when he made runs, he did so in style. The *Oxford Times* complimented Elmer Cotton on his 'pretty batting' for the county in the 1926 season.

Having finished playing for his adopted county, he was given the honour of umpiring the Oxfordshire game with the touring Indians in 1932. Throughout the 1930s and 1940s Elmer helped run the county club and became a selector.

Elmer Cotton was the driving force behind the creation of an indoor cricket school in Merton Street. In January 1926, Jack Hobbs, who then was England's most famous batsman, came down to open the school, which comprised two indoor nets. Hobbs did some coaching and then batted for half an hour. The only person to get him out was Elmer Cotton, who bowled the master batsman with a sharp off break. Just reward for his hard work in setting up Oxford's first ever coaching centre, which he ran for several winters. Elmer also worked as a coach at Magdalen College School.

Having been joined in the business by his brother Bill early on, later his son, Brian, and nephew, Elmer junior, also came to work in the shop. Not only did Elmer Cotton's shop sell equipment, but it also carried out repairs in the workshop at the back, as well as coming up with some new designs. In the 1920s, Elmer Cotton produced a new type of cricket boot, which he marketed as the 'Oxford Cricket Shoe'. Later he designed his own rugby boot, said to be the first studded rugby boot, which he advertised as the 'lightest boot in the world'. His rugby boots were worn by some of the top English rugby players, such as the speedy England and Oxford University winger Alex Obolensky.

Elmer Cotton's shop, Turl Street, Oxford.

For any local cricketer, Elmer Cotton's became the place to buy a new bat. County batsman Mike Nurton remembers the excitement of being taken by his father into Elmer Cotton's shop to buy his first cricket bat, when he was a young lad in the 1950s. Mike's dad bought him a Len Hutton autographed Gradidge bat, which cost £1 10s. Mike was thrilled, but when they got home, his mother's reaction was that £1 10s was an awful lot of money to spend on a cricket bat!

Elmer Cotton retired in the 1950s and the business was later sold, but the shop bearing his name had a very long innings, until closing in 2018.

Elmer Cotton 1881 - 1962

The Great War

War against Germany was declared in early August 1914 and the *Oxford Times* commented, 'The peaceful battles of the cricket field have now finally been overshadowed by the grim reality of actual war.' Life was suddenly turned upside down, as young men were sent across the Channel to fight for their lives.

Club cricket in Oxford ceased during the First World War, although a side called Isis was formed from those left, or stationed in the city, which played many matches, mostly against military teams.

There was a devastating loss of life during the war, with many local cricketers being killed or wounded. Like many others, the Rogers family suffered. Just one of the thousands who were killed was Herbert 'Bert' Rogers (1893 - 1916).

Bert was Peter Rogers' only son and it will come as no surprise that he followed his father's footsteps onto the cricket fields of Oxford and beyond. Bert began playing cricket for North Oxford at the St John's College ground, near to his home and where his father was groundsman.

When North Oxford beat Victoria in the Airey Cup final in 1909, 16-year-old spinner Herbert Rogers was the star, taking seven for 16. A match report concluded that, 'There is no doubt that a great future lies before young Rogers.'

Having impressed as a bowler at North Oxford, Bert Rogers moved down to Southampton and was taken onto the Hampshire ground staff. He went on to play a handful of matches for Hampshire from 1912 to 1914 but had little success. In 1914, he moved home to Worcestershire and played local cricket there, as he waited to gain a residential qualification for that county.

The outbreak of war put an end to Bert's plans, as the

beautiful cricket fields of England were soon replaced by the gruesome battlefields of France. Sadly, Lance Corporal Herbert Rogers was killed fighting at the Somme in 1916. Two of Bert's cousins were also killed in the war: one of them, William Rogers, had worked as a groundsman at Christ Church. Another cousin, Fred, who was also a groundsman, was severely wounded in the right arm, but survived.

Another poignant death with a connection to an old Oxford cricketing family was that of David James Burrin (1891-1916), who was the great nephew of the fast roundarm bowler David Burrin. Young David had held the record for the fastest swim between Folly Bridge and Iffley Lock, before emigrating to Australia in 1912. He had hoped to find a new life, but died, like many of his generation, fighting in France. The Harse family, well known for their cricket balls, also suffered when young Philip, son of Morton, was killed in France just ten days before the end of the war in November 1918.

Nearly all of the cricket clubs in and around Oxford lost some of their players during the war. A Roll of Honour printed in the *Oxford Times* in June 1919 listed 36 cricketers from Oxford clubs who had been killed, but this number would rise. At the AGM of the Cowley St John club in April 1919 it was reported that eight members had been killed and some others were still unaccounted for.

On top of all of this carnage, a number of local cricketers returned wounded, either physically or mentally. At a meeting that was held to re-establish the Cowley club in June 1919, it was reported that of the former young players that had come back from the war, one had lost a leg but still hoped to take part, whilst another had suffered severely from shell shock.

Shell shock was a new concept and only just beginning to be understood. During the war, an asylum in the village of Littlemore, on the southeastern outskirts of Oxford, was taken over by the army and used to treat soldiers who were suffering from shell shock. During and after the war, patients and staff played cricket on the ground at the hospital.

Before the outbreak of war, there had been a thriving cricket club at the Littlemore Asylum and three of its players from the pre-war years would go on to have success in the 1920s, as cricket, and life in general, returned to some form of normality.

Going Down to Southampton –
Alec Bowell and George Brown

Russell Bencraft played cricket for his St Edward's School team in the 1870s, not long after the school had moved to its new site on the Woodstock Road in the north of Oxford. He qualified as a doctor and went on to play cricket for his county. As captain, secretary and then President, Bencraft became the driving force in developing his county club as well as taking a leading role in the acquisition of a ground. That county club was Hampshire. If only Oxfordshire had such a man as Russell Bencraft, things might have turned out differently!

When they were both small fry, Oxfordshire had played a couple of friendly matches against Hampshire in 1892, but having been well beaten, Oxfordshire did not renew the fixture. Three years later, the course of these two counties diverged as Hampshire joined the first-class County Championship, whereas Oxfordshire entered what was to become the Minor Counties Championship. Not long afterwards, Hampshire recruited Horace Bowell, a young cricketer from Oxford, the first of some talented players from the city who would move south in order to play county cricket professionally.

Horace Bowell was born and raised in Jericho, a district close to the centre of Oxford, which in contrast to present times, was then a poor area. He showed early promise playing local cricket as an allrounder. As a 16-year-old, he opened the batting for Boulter Street Working Men's Institute in the 1896 final of the Airey Cup.

Quite how he came to join Hampshire is not known, but he might have chosen to go for a trial with that county because his sister Mary lived in Aldershot. Conveniently, Horace was able to stay with his sister's family for a couple of years, working as a painter and playing some cricket in the summer, whilst he served his two-year residential qualification period.

When he moved down to Hampshire, Bowell dropped the name Horace and called himself Alec (one of his middle names was Alexander). Having secured a place in the Hampshire team towards the end of the 1902 season, he worked his way up the batting order to become an opener. A small, nimble man, he was also a sprightly cover fielder.

Hampshire batsman Alec Bowell.

In September 1904, after he had just completed his third season in first-class cricket with Hampshire, Alec Bowell came back to Oxford and played a friendly game for the St Thomas club against Littlemore Asylum. Batting at number 4 for the Asylum team that day was a tall 16-year-old lad named George Brown, who was making his debut. It was not a successful first game for Brown, as he was bowled by Alec Bowell with just a single run to his name.

Perhaps seeing Alec Bowell, a young working-class man from Oxford, become a professional cricketer inspired George Brown to follow in his footsteps. Five years later, George Brown would make his debut in first-class county cricket in the same Hampshire side as Alec Bowell.

George Brown was a Temple Cowley boy. He worked as an attendant at the Littlemore Asylum, where he also played cricket. By the end of the 1906 season, he was showing promise as a wicketkeeper and forceful batsman, whose approach was to 'hit it hard and often', according to one local reporter.

Somehow, George got an interview for a job on the Hampshire CCC ground staff, but with little money in his pocket, he had the problem of how to get to Southampton. Remarkably, he decided to walk the 60-odd miles to the interview, which was in February/early March, so could have been in bad weather. It must have taken him at least a couple of days, but the Brown family were made of sturdy stuff, as George's brother Fred did something similar when he set off to walk to Birmingham to find work as a bricklayer. The determination of both of them paid off, as Fred found work in Coventry on his walk up to the Midlands and George was taken on by Hampshire.

At Hampshire, in the seasons leading up to the First World War, Brown discarded his wicketkeeping gloves and developed into a fast-bowling allrounder, as well as gaining the reputation of being one of the finest fielders in the country. His bowling action was unusual, with a whirlwind of arms, but on his day he could be dynamic: when George took six wickets at Worcester in 1909, the *Yorkshire Evening Post* described how the home side had 'quite collapsed to Brown's fast, eccentric deliveries'.

Both Brown and Bowell came through the First World War unscathed. After the war George Brown was given some opportunities by Hampshire to open the batting with Alec Bowell and in 1920 they had a record opening partnership of 204 against Worcestershire, when both scored centuries. Their finest opening partnership was in the same season, against county champions Yorkshire at Headingley, when they put on 183 in just two hours and ten minutes. A crowd of over 18,000 Yorkshire folk watched in dismay as Bowell scored 95, with Brown going on to make an undefeated 232, as Hampshire gained a shock victory.

Alec Bowell played for Hampshire up until 1927, by which time he was 46 years old, and his tally of over 18,000 runs for the county puts him 11th in the list of their all-time first-class run-scorers. After retiring from professional cricket, he moved back to Oxford, did some coaching, became a publican and then a shopkeeper in the south of the city. In retirement from the professional game, Alec played the odd game of cricket in Oxford, sometimes with his son Norman, in the Oxford City side.

George Brown was a brave, attacking, left-handed batsman who 'hooked and drove with furious strength', according to the renowned cricket writer John Arlott. When the Australian fast bowlers Gregory and McDonald were terrifying English batsmen in the 1921 Ashes series, Brown was called up for the third Test at Headingley, as a wicketkeeper-batsman. Going into bat with the score at 67 for five, George scored a half-century in his first innings, helping England to avoid the follow on and then top-scored when promoted to open the batting in the second. Alas, England lost that game, but they managed to draw the last two Tests, with George Brown continuing to bat at the top of the order and seeing off the Aussie fast men. He averaged 50 in three Tests that summer and also impressed with his wicketkeeping, despite hardly ever having kept wicket for his county. Failure to score many runs on matting wickets on a subsequent tour to South Africa brought an end to his England career, however, after just seven Test matches.

The highlight of George Brown's Hampshire career came in 1922, in a game at Edgbaston against Warwickshire. Having dismissed the home side for 223, Hampshire were then bowled out within nine overs for the meagre total of 15! Alec Bowell and George Brown were amongst eight Hampshire batsmen who failed to score. Following on, Hampshire turned the tide by making 521, including a magnificent 172 from George Brown, and went on to win the game.

Brown was in great batting form in 1926 and with the Test series against Australia level, he was selected for the final Test at the Oval, again as a wicketkeeper-batsman. Cruelly, he broke a finger in a county game days before the match. He thus missed out on playing for his country again and Ashes glory.

George Brown batting for England.

Although taking his cricket seriously, George had a sense of humour. There is a tale that when batting against the Nottinghamshire fast bowlers Larwood and Voce, he was hit on the ear by a rising ball, just before lunch. As a joke, he came out to bat after the lunch break wearing a motorcyclist's helmet. An alternative version of the story claimed that he was wearing a padded women's hat. Whatever it was, it raised a few laughs. A young 'Lofty' Herman later played with George and remembered having a lot of fun with him and his fellow professionals.

Towards the end of his career, George Brown became Hampshire's regular wicketkeeper, which was arduous for a man in his forties, as he also opened the batting and was playing six days a week.

George Brown had a very eventful, if inconsistent career, but his allround contributions for Hampshire and England were impressive. A combative batsman, never afraid to taunt and take on the fastest of bowlers, he is third in the all-time list of Hampshire first-class run-scorers with nearly 23,000 runs. On top of that he was a tireless fast bowler, Test match standard wicketkeeper and one of the finest fielders of his generation. All of this whilst suffering from hernias throughout his career which forced him to wear a form of girdle. Writing in 1963, John Arlott stated that George Brown was the most complete allround cricketer the game had ever known. That is some claim! Arlott was a Hampshire man, which probably influenced his judgement, but George Brown could certainly bat, bowl, field and keep wicket to a high standard ... there has never been an English cricketer quite like him.

Not only did George Brown have the skills, but he also had the bravado. He was a special cricketer. 'Uninhibited, combative, physically superb', to quote Arlott. George was probably born in the wrong era, as he would have been well suited to the modern limited overs game and the 'Bazball' approach to Test cricket!

Both Alec Bowell and George Brown showed that at the start of the 20th century, it was possible to make the huge leap from playing for small clubs in Oxford to becoming professionals in first-class cricket. They were helped by having to fulfil what in effect was a two-year apprenticeship whilst they served their residential qualification, but they illustrated that whatever your background, if you were determined, you could make it as a professional county cricketer.

Both were to have sadness later in their lives. George Brown's only son, Edwin, had a spell on the Hampshire ground staff, but he never played professionally. Sadly, he was killed in a German bombing raid on Southampton in 1940.

Alec Bowell also had one son, Norman, who was born in Oxford. Having worked as a merchant seaman in the early 1920s, Norman Bowell played a couple of first-class games for Hampshire, before moving back to Oxford. He joined the City club, for whom he played up until the outbreak of war and he also made a handful of appearances for Oxfordshire. Norman had led an untroubled life, but the outbreak of war saw him join the army as a gunner. He was captured by the Japanese in Singapore, suffered badly and was eventually killed in horrific circumstances, when held prisoner on a South Seas island in 1943.

Earning his Money

As a young boy, George Brown was sometimes keener on playing cricket on Cowley Marsh than doing the jobs that his father gave him, such as mucking out the pigs. One day, as a punishment, his father broke up the small cricket bat that George had made for himself, when he discovered that his son had neglected his tasks in order to go out and play on Cowley Marsh. He chided George, telling him that playing cricket 'would never put dinner on the table'.

George went on to prove his father wrong, but in his early years as a cricketer, he could not afford to eat any fancy dinners. When he was taken onto the ground staff at Hampshire's Northlands Road ground in Southampton, for the summer of 1907, George was paid 25s a week. A very modest wage, but he found lodgings at Mr Bennett's house near to the ground, at a cost of 5s a week, so he still had £1 in his pocket to live off.

George became a professional at Hampshire in 1909 and like the other pros, was paid on a match basis. For an away game he received £6 a match, but the professionals had to pay for their own travel (usually a third-class rail ticket) and accommodation out of that fee. By contrast, the amateurs in the team would be booked into an hotel and given travelling expenses for a first-class train ticket!

Being paid match by match, there was an incentive for the professionals to keep fit, play through injuries and perform well. By 1910, the Hampshire Committee began to provide some remuneration to injured players, but not much. When George missed a game that season due to injury, the committee paid him £1, but told him that this would not set a precedent for the future!

By 1912, Hampshire had started paying 'talent money' for fielding. Being the best fielder in the side, George Brown was paid the highest, but that was only £3 for the whole season! Talent money payments were also made for 50s, 100s and five wickets. George Brown and the prolific batsman Phil Mead would usually be at the top of the list and in 1920 they earned £28 each.

In pre-war times, George did not receive any pay from Hampshire in the close season and found work in Southampton docks most winters. When cricket resumed after the war, the professionals at Hampshire were able to negotiate better deals. They obtained £70 winter pay for 1919/20 but had to sign an agreement committing themselves to Hampshire.

By 1920, the Hampshire pros were being paid £8 for a home match and £10 for an away game, as well as having their rail fare paid. The pay of cricketers at this time was roughly similar to professional footballers. There was a maximum wage in the Football League, which in 1921 was reduced to £8 a week during the season and £6 a week during the 15-week close season. So the maximum that a professional footballer could officially earn was £386. George Brown would have been earning about £330 a year at this time, but he was still on the way up and not at a wealthy county. It took a long time, but the wages of professional English cricketers and footballers subsequently diverged dramatically, due firstly to the abolition of football's minimum wage in the 1960s and then in recent times to the advent of Sky television and the Premier League.

When it came to negotiating pay rates in the early 20th century, professionals were in a weak position, as they could not move to another club without taking two years out of county cricket. The growth of league cricket in the north of England gave talented county pros some bargaining power and George Brown used this to his advantage. In September 1920, Accrington, in the Lancashire League, reportedly offered him a five-year contract at £500 a year, talent money, a house, winter employment and a benefit! This must have been very tempting, but George stayed on at Hampshire, after an agreement with the Committee that when he had a benefit, he would be guaranteed £1,000.

In 1923, George and four of his fellow professionals asked the Hampshire Committee for guaranteed minimum pay and after negotiations, a minimum summer wage of £200 was agreed. Half pay when missing a game through injury was also introduced by Hampshire, so things were moving in the right direction for their professional cricketers.

It would be another four decades before a cricketers' union was formed, but many of the professional cricketers of the 1920s had empathy with fellow manual workers. There was a General Strike in 1926, led by the miners, but it did not go well and caused great distress in mining communities. In September 1926, a letter appeared in the *Oxford Chronicle*, signed by several leading cricketers, including Jack Hobbs and Harold Larwood. The letter was an appeal to British sportsmen, 'for help to the wives and children of the miners, who are the real victims of the great industrial struggle now going on'. The touring Australian cricket team donated an autographed bat to be sold for the benefit of the appeal fund.

Being given a benefit was crucial to the financial security of a professional cricketer. George Brown was awarded a benefit by Hampshire in 1926 and with the help of his guaranteed £1,000, he was able to purchase a plot of land in Chandlers Ford and build a handsome detached house.

Playing for England did not make you rich in the 1920s, but it did enhance your reputation and for several winters George Brown was able to get overseas coaching jobs, first in South Africa and then India. He also went on an arduous MCC tour to India and Ceylon in 1926/27, but with limited finances at MCC, he was only paid £300 for six months' hard graft on that tour.

Jack Newman had begun playing for Hampshire shortly before George Brown and the two of them were best friends. Newman had given sterling service, bowling over 96,000 deliveries in his 21 seasons at the county, until he developed heart problems in 1931. At the end of the season, he was not given a new contract, and in an instant, his cricket career was over. It was both a tough life and a precarious one for a county pro, with no job security.

With an economic depression in the early 1930s, wages of workers fell, including those of professional cricketers. For the 1934 season, George was offered terms of £6 10s for a home game and £8 10s for an away game, which was much less than he was being paid in 1920.

With an aching body, George Brown rejected the offered terms and decided to retire. To mark his long service to Hampshire, a testimonial fund was set up, from which he received £292. At the age of 47 he had to find a new way of making a living and like many other ex-professionals, he became a pub landlord. George also had a couple of seasons as an umpire in the County Championship, but he did not have the calm temperament needed for umpiring and was stood down for giving too many lbw decisions.

In later years George did some coaching jobs. By the 1950s he was living in a modest terraced house in Winchester and his last job was as a car park attendant. Once, when the coach of the touring Australian team called in at his Winchester car park, George wore his old England blazer to work, to catch the Aussies' eye. He was very proud of having played cricket for England.

George Brown was 'penny wise and pound foolish', according to his grandson Dave Strong and he had limited means in his later years, when he was dogged by ill health: but the game of cricket had given the Temple Cowley lad some exciting times and enabled him to travel the world. From a young age, George had been passionate about cricket, and it seems that he cared as much about the game as the amount of money in his pocket.

Alec Bowell 1880 - 1957
First-class 1902 - 1927 475 matches
18,509 runs @ 24.1

George Brown 1887 - 1964
First-class 1908 - 1933 612 matches
25,649 runs @ 26.7 & 626 wickets @ 29.8
646 dismissals (567 ct 79 st)

7 England Test caps
299 runs @ 29.8

Tom Shepherd – Run-Scorer

The small village of Headington Quarry, located to the east of Oxford, was known for the stone that it produced to build Oxford colleges. In 1889, Tom Shepherd was born in the village. His father worked in a local brickworks and then became a builder, but when Tom left school, he took a job as a gardener.

Shepherd showed early promise as a cricketer, playing for the Headington Quarry village team. In 1908, he batted well in the Headington Quarry side that won the Telegraph Cup, which was a competition for smaller clubs in and around Oxford. The following season he had the impressive batting average of 41 for Quarry and the *Oxford Times* commented, 'Shepherd has a very watchful defence and with more experience will develop scoring strokes that should enable him to make a big name of himself.' Playing for Headington Quarry, Shepherd somehow came to the notice of Surrey, and he went for a trial at The Oval. Unfortunately, he was told to come back in a few years' time.

In 1912 Shepherd joined the Littlemore Asylum club and had a remarkable season for them, making five centuries as he scored over 1,000 runs at an average of 74. He was asked to play as a guest for Oxford City in some mid-week games and scored well.

Tom continued to plunder runs for Littlemore Asylum in the following two years, making many more centuries. He finished the 1914 season with an astonishing average of 106 for the Asylum, which was not noted for having a flat wicket.

After the war, Shepherd took Surrey's advice and went back for another trial in 1919. This time he was taken on as a professional, but by now he was 29 years old. He took a couple of seasons to settle in, but blossomed in 1921, scoring heavily as he established himself as a middle order batsman in the Surrey side. He had an appetite for scoring runs and could be prolific. In successive matches in 1921 he scored 212 against Lancashire and then 210 not out against Kent.

Shepherd had a sound defence, was a fine front foot driver of the ball and according to *The Cricketer,* 'Few batsmen have ever punished a loose ball with more unfailing certainty and power.' He let his batting do his talking, as he was a quiet man and rarely showed his emotions.

Tom Shepherd.

Shepherd's finest season was 1927, when he scored over 2,000 runs and played in Test Trials. In a game against Gloucestershire at The Oval that year he made a breathtaking 277 not out. Next day, he followed that by recording his best ever bowling figures of six for 78, with his medium paced bowling. Despite Shepherd's efforts, Gloucestershire escaped with a draw, thanks to a couple of centuries from Wally Hammond.

Shepherd played for Surrey up until 1932, finishing with an impressive career batting average of just a shade under 40. As the *Oxford Times* had predicted back in 1908, Tom Shepherd had indeed made a 'big name' for himself in cricket.

Coming back to Headington

Way before Tom Shepherd's time, cricket was a popular game in Headington and Headington Quarry. Both villages had cricket clubs in the 1840s, but like elsewhere, over the years, these clubs would come and go out of existence.

Tom Shepherd's mother was from the well-known Coppock family, members of which had been enthusiastic cricketers over previous generations. Back in 1849, there was a veteran batsman named George Coppock playing for Quarry, whilst there were five Coppocks who played in a Married v Single game in Headington Quarry in 1860. Three years later, it was reported that Mr G Coppock of The Six Bells in Headington Quarry beat Mr W Gibbons of The Cricketers, Cowley, in a single wicket match, to win a leg of mutton with trimmings. If you were good at cricket in that era, you could earn your Sunday lunch!

By 1876 there were enough cricketers for both villages to have second teams, which played each other in August that year in a match at the Britannia Inn ground, in Headington. Things could often get feisty in matches between Headington and Quarry, but following the advent of the Airey Cup competition, the teams combined for cup ties. This proved successful when Headington United won the Airey Cup in 1902, with the two best Quarry players, Cox and Coppock, in the team.

After Tom Shepherd left the Quarry club in 1911, both the Headington and Headington Quarry clubs soon folded. A new team called Titup Wanderers was established in 1914, which was renamed Titup United when cricket restarted in 1919. Having begun playing in a field off Old Road, where the grass in the outfield was long and the dandelions plentiful, the Titup team moved to the Trinity College ground in Oxford in 1922.

Throughout the 1920s, Tom Shepherd was always keen to return home to Headington and play games in September, after Surrey's fixtures had been completed. He was not a man for taking it easy in club cricket. In September 1921 Tom scored an undefeated 115 for Titup United against Victoria. A year later, he played in two games for Titup United against Thame, taking seven wickets in the first match and scoring 113 not out in the second.

Very occasionally, things did not go Shepherd's way. In September 1922, he played for Mr F Lee's Eleven, at Horspath. After the village side was dismissed for the meagre total of 36, drama unfolded as Tom Shepherd was soon trapped lbw and his team mates then capitulated as the Lee team was all out for just 23. It would be reasonable to assume that the Horspath pitch was then not very reliable!

Titup United changed its name to Headington United in 1923 but continued to play on the Trinity College ground. Tom Shepherd returned home again in September of 1923 and also 1924, to score many more runs for Headington.

In an effort to find their own ground, the Headington United football and cricket clubs set up a company called the Headington Sports Ground Ltd and this raised money to buy a plot of land. By 1925, a new ground had been acquired and laid out, which meant that Headington United could begin playing cricket again in its home village. In 1925 the Headington New Sports Ground in Manor Road was opened with a match against Oxford City CC. Sixty years later, as the home of Oxford United FC, this Manor ground would host First Division football.

In October 1926, it was reported that Tom Shepherd scored a 'magnificent' century in a game at Blenheim Palace. By then, having played mostly for Headington United, since early September he had scored over 600 runs in local cricket, at an average in excess of 100, as well as taking over 30 wickets!

Tom continued to chalk up the runs whenever he came back to Oxford, such as in September 1928, when he made a score of 165 not out for Headington. That month Shepherd was one of seven Surrey players in Mr A Kempston's team that played a match against Oxford City, in which he scored 126. In September 1929 Tom assembled his own strong side, to travel out to the east of Oxford to play the small village of Tiddington. He scored 96 and took some wickets as his side defeated Tiddington by 150 runs. No letting up there! Whether it was for Surrey, Headington or any other team, Tom Shepherd just loved scoring runs.

The following September he took five wickets and made 117 for Headington against Tiddington. By the end of the month Tom had scored four centuries for Headington at an average of 129! Not many other batsmen could get a look in.

Tom Shepherd was given a benefit by Surrey in 1931 and when Headington played a re-formed Titup in the Airey Cup that year, a bat signed by the Australians was raffled at the match, with the proceeds going to Tom's benefit. He had a lot of admirers, friends and relatives in Headington to buy tickets.

Despite his close ties with Headington, Tom remained in London when he retired from playing for Surrey in 1932, working in later life as a groundsman and coach. He was a top-quality batsman, with his talent matched by a very strong desire to score runs, no matter whether he was batting at The Oval or Tiddington.

Tom Shepherd 1889 - 1957
First-class 1919 - 1932 363 matches
18,715 runs @ 39.8 & 445 wickets @ 30.7

Charlie Walters – County Stalwart

Your father can have a big influence on your life and that was certainly the case for Charlie Walters. His dad, Jon, was a very keen local cricketer and his enthusiasm for the game rubbed off on Charlie.

Jon Walters lived in the village of Littlemore and worked at the local asylum, where he became the Head Attendant. He was a founder member of the Littlemore Asylum CC in 1886 and played for them up until 1914. In his first 25 seasons for the club up to 1910, it is known that he took 1,538 wickets at an average of just over six, with a batting average of about 20. Impressive figures! Jon was a canny seam bowler. 'There are still few bowlers more difficult than Walters when the pitch assists him,' commented the *Oxford Times* in 1909, after he had taken six for nine against Pembroke College.

Jon Walters had six sons, but the eldest, Arthur, had just started playing cricket with his father in the Asylum team when he drowned in a nearby lake in 1906. Another son, Chris, became a top order batsman in the Asylum side and finally young Charlie Walters played the odd game with his father for the Asylum and also the Sandford village team, just before the outbreak of war in 1914. Charlie showed early promise and was asked to play in an Oxford City trial match for a Colts side against the City A team in July 1914, but failed to make a score.

Charlie Walters was enlisted into the army in 1916 but came through the war unharmed and on his return began playing football for Oxford City Reserves at the start of the 1919/20 season. Described in a newspaper report as a 'hefty young half back', Charlie was moved up to the City first team in October 1919. A few weeks later he impressed in some trial matches for Tottenham Hotspur Reserves and in mid-December signed as a professional for the north London club. It had been a swift rise from the White House

Ground to White Hart Lane!

Charlie became a centre half and with him at the heart of their defence, Spurs reached the FA Cup Final in 1921. The final was played at Stamford Bridge, in front of a crowd of about 73,000, which included the King and some members of the touring Australian cricket team. With torrential rain creating large pools of water, it was a scrappy game, but in the wet and mud, Spurs beat Wolverhampton Wanders 1-0. Charlie was a 'tower of strength' in the final, but he was a modest man and the cup triumph did not go to his head.

Charlie Walters.

Charlie came back to Oxford at the end of the football season and in the summer of 1921 played for the Cowley side that won the Oxford Cricket League. The following year, after a guest appearance for his old Littlemore team, Charlie joined

Oxford City, where he scored runs consistently. He was an attacking batsman, sometimes too attacking according to the *Athletic News*, which commented that, 'Walters looks like developing into a fine cricketer when he can cure himself of the desire to have a go.' Just like his father, Charlie was also a clever medium paced seam bowler.

Amidst renewed enthusiasm, a new Oxfordshire County Cricket Club was established in 1922. After impressing in a trial game, Charlie was selected for Oxfordshire's first Minor Counties match against Cambridgeshire. He made a solid contribution as Oxfordshire triumphed and became a regular in the county side for the rest of the season ... in fact for many, many seasons.

Charlie scored 220 not out for Oxfordshire against Bedfordshire in 1924, which is still a county record, sharing a partnership of 331 for the second wicket with his skipper, the old Etonian Brocas Burrows. This remains the highest-ever partnership for the county. Despite these great deeds, Oxfordshire only drew.

Charlie played most of his club cricket for Oxford City, but also turned out for Cowley and other teams. He also played for the Tottenham Hotspur cricket side and missed an Oxfordshire game in 1924 because he was playing cricket for Spurs. In October 1926, Charlie moved football clubs, joining Second Division Fulham. He starred for the Fulham cricket team which won the Evening News Cricket Cup the following summer, knocking out Spurs along the way!

Charlie was a leading member of the Oxfordshire side throughout the 1920s. In 1929, he played a prominent part as the county won all but one of its matches, often by wide margins, to win the Minor Counties Championship. As an example of his allround contribution, in a ten-wicket victory over Cambridgeshire that season, Charlie scored a half-century and had match figures of six for 44 in 34 overs, with the *Oxford Times* commenting that, 'He seems to be able to pitch the ball with mechanical precision.'

When Buckinghamshire, the runners up, played Oxfordshire in a challenge match at the end of the season, Charlie took six wickets in Bucks' first innings as Oxfordshire won comfortably. He finished top of the county bowling averages in that 1929 season, taking 54 wickets at a cost of only ten runs apiece.

There are stories that Charlie Walters had offers from first-class counties to play as a professional, but he never took these up. Although initially playing for Oxfordshire as an amateur, so valuable was he to the team that he was made the club's senior professional. In 1931, he was also given a benefit by the county, but two games organised as part of the benefit, against a Jack Parsons' Eleven, were poorly attended. Charlie also earned money by coaching, becoming the Oxford University coach in the late 1920s, where he became very popular with the students. The money that he made from cricket was always secondary to his main income, which he earned as a travelling salesman.

Consistent allround performances for Oxfordshire led to Charlie being selected for four first-class Minor Counties representative matches. Disappointingly, Charlie made a duck in his only innings against the New Zealanders in one of these games in 1931. Nevertheless, Charlie became the third cricketer from the Littlemore Asylum club, following George Brown and Tom Shepherd, to have played first-class cricket. His father would have been a proud man.

Throughout the early 1930s Charlie consistently topped Oxfordshire's bowling averages, although his batting form started to decline. By 1939, he was still bowling well both for Oxford City and Oxfordshire, once again topping the bowling averages for the county. Charlie had continued to play as a professional for Oxfordshire throughout the 1930s, although he was not paid much, as the club finances were in a poor state.

When cricket resumed in 1946, Charlie continued to play for Oxford City and even had a few more games for Oxfordshire, for whom he also served as a selector. After a 25-year stint, Charlie finished as the Oxford University coach in 1953, but continued to coach youngsters at Oxford City, where he became the club President. Charlie had a lifetime of cricket in Oxford and was held in high regard. Back in 1921, they thought a lot of him in the London borough of Tottenham as well.

Charlie Walters 1897 - 1971
First-class 1930 - 1934 4 matches

Minor Counties Championship 1922 - 1952 154 matches
5,006 runs @ 23.5 & 513 wickets @ 15.9

Morris Motors Men – Johnny Arnold and 'Lofty' Herman

The rapid growth of the motor industry in Cowley during the 1920s and 1930s had a major impact on Oxford. For centuries, it had remained a rather genteel, sleepy, inward-looking city, dominated by its university. Up until the First World War, such was the influence of the University, with its extensive property ownership and wealth, that nothing much changed in Oxford without its approval. As a result, nothing much changed. But in the inter-war years, there was dramatic innovation, as industrialisation transformed the east of the city, with the building of large car factories and sprawling housing estates. There was also a large influx of workers who came from other less affluent areas, such as South Wales, to find employment in the new car factories. All of this change was instigated by the efforts of an ingenious Oxford man named William Morris.

Morris had started off making bicycles in the 1890s but moved on to selling and repairing cars from premises nestling amongst the colleges, in Longwall Street. He then began making cars, with his famous two-seater Bullnose being assembled at a factory that he set up at the vacant former Military College in Cowley in 1913. The Morris Motors Car Company was established in 1919 and within a few years became a major car manufacturer, creating thousands of jobs and making William Morris a very wealthy man.

With war having ended in November 1918, cricket in Oxford restarted the following summer. Nearly all of the pre-war clubs re-formed, but there was a new entry in the Oxford League that year ... the Morris Motors works team.

The company laid out a new sports facility in Cowley, with football and cricket clubs being set up for its employees. The Morris Motors Cricket Club quickly established itself and in 1922 reached the play-off final of the Oxford and District League, only to lose to Oxford City.

In 1924, two young lads who worked together in the paint shop at the car works began playing cricket together for the Morris Motors Second Eleven. Their names were Johnny Arnold and Oswald Herman.

Herman had grown up on a farm, on the outskirts of the village of Horspath, just to the east of Oxford. He came from an old farming family, who had showed some interest in cricket. As far back as 1868, there is a report of Horspath playing a match against Summertown in a field lent by Mr Bernard Herman, who was Oswald's grandfather. Two of Bernard Herman's teenage sons batted at the bottom of the order for Horspath in that game.

Oswald had played some cricket when at the Central School in Oxford and grew to be a tall, thin lad. He was an allrounder and in 1925 took ten wickets in the two innings final of the Under 21s Telegraph Cup, but this could not prevent Summertown defeating Morris Motors.

Herman's development as a cricketer went largely unnoticed. In 1926 he was still playing for Morris Motors in the second division of the league, often opening the batting. The following year, his accurate seam bowling made an impression at a trial for the Hampshire CCC nursery, which he was asked to join in May 1927. The Oxfordshire selectors had been caught on the hop by Herman's swift progression, although when he played a game for Oxfordshire against Monmouthshire in 1927, he only took a solitary wicket and scored one run.

Batsman Johnny Arnold was a Temple Cowley lad. His father Fred had been a wicketkeeper-batsman, playing for Cowley and as a professional for Oxfordshire, whilst working as a groundsman at places such as Radley College and the Parks. In contrast to Oswald Herman, even as a schoolboy, Johnny Arnold had gained a reputation as being a bright prospect. From 1925 onwards he played mainly for

Cowley, scoring both heavily and stylishly, and it was not long before Hampshire showed an interest.

In their younger days, both of them also played football for Cowley, where Oswald was a centre half and Johnny a left winger. Arnold went on to join Oxford City FC and soon became a crowd favourite at the White House ground. He moved to Hampshire in 1928 to start a two-year residential qualification for the county cricket club and very conveniently, found winter employment by signing as a professional footballer for Second Division Southampton FC.

Having served their residential qualification periods, Herman began playing County Championship cricket for Hampshire in 1929, as did Arnold a year later. Johnny came back to play for Oxfordshire in 1929 and scored prolifically as the county won the Minor Counties Championship for the first time. Reporting on a century that Arnold made against Cambridgeshire that year the *Oxford Times* predicted that 'he should go far, as he has a level head.' Johnny also made his first-class debut for Hampshire against the touring South Africans that season.

Because of his height, Oswald Herman soon acquired the nickname 'Lofty'. He had the ability to swing the ball into the batsman and became the workhorse of the Hampshire bowling line-up in the 1930s.

Johnny Arnold made an immediate impact at Hampshire, so much so that after a successful first season in county cricket in 1930, he was picked to play for England in a Test match against New Zealand in 1931. His rise from Oxfordshire to England had been swift. On the eve of his Test debut, the *Oxford Times* wrote in praise of both Johnny and his father Fred:

> It used to be said of all boys born in Cowley that they came into this world with a bat in their hands. That was in the days when the Rogers, the Kings, the Burrins and the Bancalaris were the backbone of the Cowley side.

Today the descendants have not quite kept up the village reputation, but that the species has not entirely died out is proved by the selection of Johnny Arnold for England against New Zealand tomorrow.

Thirty years or more ago Fred Arnold kept wicket for Cowley and Oxfordshire and was a hitter who had few superiors. A man of powerful physique, he was marked down by one of the first-class counties – unless my memory plays me false it was Kent – but he would not qualify for them. Cricket in Johnny's case is therefore hereditary. There have never been any doubts in the minds of the best judges that the boy would go far, as combined with a good style, a fit body and a level head, he is fully equipped for the profession he has adopted. He is a natural games player who, largely through will power and assiduous practice, has placed himself well up on the ladder of sports fame. He has brought credit to himself, to his family and not least to the county of his birth.

Johnny opened the batting against New Zealand along with another Test debutant, Fred Bakewell, a 22-year-old Northamptonshire batsman. Although born in Walsall, Bakewell had moved to Oxford and as a young lad both he and Johnny had played in the Oxford Schools Cricket Scheme. This scheme had been set up in the city in 1921, whereby several colleges provided their grounds for elementary schools to play on, as well as students to do some coaching. Such sporting generosity by the colleges to the children of the city was ground-breaking. The scheme proved a success and Fred Bakewell, who stood out for his brilliant fielding, and Johnny Arnold, who impressed with his batting, were just two of the youngsters who benefited from it.

Unfortunately Johnny Arnold made a duck in his first Test innings and, despite scoring 34 in the second, never played another Test match. Unlike Arnold, Bakewell was given more opportunities for England and scored a thrilling century against the West Indies in 1933, finishing with a

Johnny Arnold. Double international wearing his Oxfordshire cap.

test average of 45. Off the field, things did not go so well for Fred, as he led a troubled life, making many appearances before the judiciary and having three serious car accidents.

Meanwhile, Arnold's football career thrived and despite playing on the wing, he scored 46 goals for Southampton in 106 league games, before being sold to Fulham in 1933. Shortly afterwards, he played for England in a defeat by Scotland at Hampden Park. This was to be his only international match and thus Johnny Arnold played just once for England at both football and cricket.

Arnold was a classy, attacking batsman, not afraid to take on fast bowling and he gained a reputation for plundering off spin. On his day, Johnny could be scintillating, and he scored heavily for Hampshire in the 1930s. He had a poor run of form in 1938 and at the end of that season it was announced that both Arnold and Herman were leaving Hampshire. Johnny Arnold had a change of heart and stayed on, but Lofty went off to play a season of league cricket in 1939.

After the war, when county cricket resumed in the 1946 season, Lofty Herman and Johnny Arnold played well for

Hampshire, and also for a few years more. Lofty started to bowl off cutters and off spin late in his career, but by the time he retired from first-class cricket in 1948, he had taken over 1,000 wickets for Hampshire, one of only seven bowlers to have done so. He then played three seasons of Minor Counties cricket, two of them for Wiltshire. Johnny Arnold finished at Hampshire in 1950 and also had a prolific career, being fifth in the all-time list of Hampshire run-scorers with over 21,000 first-class runs.

In the 1950s, Herman worked for several years as a cricket coach, at such diverse places as Harrow School, Butlin's holiday camps and in South Africa. It says a lot about the prominence of cricket in the 1950s that it was popular amongst the state school children who holidayed at Butlin's. Towards the other end of the scale, Lofty was also employed at Oxford University to coach in the early season nets and assess the capabilities of new players.

Johnny Arnold hitting out.

In 1963, Lofty Herman began umpiring in the County Championship, joining Johnny Arnold, who had become a first-class umpire two years earlier. Both went on to have successful careers, being well-regarded by the players. They sometimes umpired together, the last occasion being in the Sussex v Indians match in 1971, not long before they both hung up their white coats.

Lofty Herman's son Bob became a professional cricketer in the 1960s, joining Middlesex, rather than his father's county. Bob recalls that, rather surprisingly, his father was appointed to umpire a couple of Championship matches in which he played. Lofty managed to avoid giving his son out, which was just as well, as his wife had told him not to bother coming home if he did! Bob later joined Hampshire and was an important seam bowler in their side that won the County Championship in 1973.

Bob Herman also remembers his father complaining about the standard of the fielding of the amateur cricketers that he played with in the 1930s. According to Lofty, the amateurs were poor fielders and if the ball went past them, they did not bother to chase it, much to the detriment of his bowling figures!

In 1970, Oxfordshire played Worcestershire in the first round of the Gillette Cup. Lofty Herman umpired this match, and it must have brought back memories for him, as the game was played at the Morris Motors ground, where he had started playing club cricket nearly half a century before. Lofty loved the game of cricket and made a name for himself as a player, coach and then umpire, spending most of his working life in the game.

Lofty Herman and Johnny Arnold had a lot in common, having worked side by side in a car factory, played together in Oxford and at Hampshire CCC, and on the odd occasion, umpired together. One thing that they did not have in common was their height, because at 6ft 4in, Lofty loomed high over 5ft 7in Johnny.

Lofty Herman coaching at Butlins.

Johnny Arnold 1907 - 1984
First class 1929 - 1950 402 matches
21,831 runs @ 32.8

1 England Test cap

Oswald 'Lofty' Herman 1907 - 1987
First class 1929 - 1948 322 matches
1,045 wickets @ 27.0 & 4,336 runs @ 11.1

The Next Generations of the Rogers Family –
The Inter-War Years

'Len' Rogers

When Peter and 'Brusher' Rogers retired from playing cricket, the baton, or rather the bat, passed on to the next generation of the Rogers family.

'Brusher' Rogers and his wife Bertha had four sons, the second oldest being Joseph Leonard, who was known as 'Len'. On leaving school Len's first job was as a golf caddy at Cowley Marsh, but he soon showed promise as a cricketer. When only 17 years old, he scored plenty of runs for Cowley in the 1914 season. With his aggressive batting, he also scored quickly, making an undefeated 163 for Cowley against the Cowley Barracks that year, in just 80 minutes!

Having served in the army and survived the war, Len returned home in 1919 and began working in Elmer Cotton's shop. He initially played for Cowley, before joining Oxford City in 1920. By then he had developed into an allrounder, one newspaper describing him as 'a splendid bat, good bowler and a wonderfully keen fielder'. Following a couple of successful years as the groundsman/professional at Abingdon Pavlova, he then joined Morris Motors.

Rogers began playing for Oxfordshire when the county club was set up in 1922 but did not establish himself in the county team as an allrounder until the 1928 season. That year his Morris Motors team won the Oxfordshire League for the third time in four years and in the final Len had a dramatic impact. Remarkably, the league final against Clarendon Press was played over three days, which at that time was the same duration as Test matches! Making the most of the time available, Len scored 200 not out in the second innings, having defended well early on, before batting like a 'dashing adventurer', according to the *Oxford Times*.

Len played in the Oxfordshire team that won the Minor Counties Championship in 1929. In one county game against Bedfordshire that season he struck the ball out of the ground three times in an innings of 94. 'There is no finer hitter than Rogers,' commented the *Oxford Times*.

Having won the Minor Counties Championship in 1929, Oxfordshire played a challenge match against second-placed Buckinghamshire at the Merton College ground at the end of the season. One of the spectators at that game was Brusher Rogers. Having toiled in unsuccessful Oxfordshire sides during his playing days, Brusher must have been gratified to see his son Len play in a team that finally lifted the Minor Counties trophy.

Len's last appearance for Oxfordshire was in 1934, but he continued playing for Morris Motors. He made the headlines with his attacking batting in 1937, scoring a century in only 41 minutes for Morris Motors against Bedfordshire Club and Ground. Even by Len's standards, that was some hitting! After the war, Len continued playing for Morris Motors, as did his son Terry, who also made one appearance for Oxfordshire in 1949.

Len Rogers was an allround sportsman, being a scratch golfer and talented footballer. He was a speedy, bustling centre forward who made good use of the shoulder charge. He scored regularly for the strong Cowley side, and in the autumn of 1920 played as a trialist for Tottenham Hotspur Reserves. Nothing came of the trial, but he had success with Cowley, which in 1922/23 won the triple of the Oxfordshire Senior Cup, the Oxfordshire Charity Cup and the Oxfordshire Senior League.

Len moved to Oxford City FC, where he continued to score goals. In March 1925, Oxford City beat a strong Tottenham Hotspur side by four goals to two in a friendly at the White House Ground. Len scored all four of City's goals, which was one in the eye for the club that had rejected him. He only played 57 matches for Oxford City, but netted 54 goals, a fantastic strike rate.

Len was popular, with many friends. He was very much a Cowley man and never moved away, working in later life as a lorry driver.

Len Rogers 1897 - 1981
Minor Counties Championship 1922 - 1934 50 matches
1,545 runs @ 20.6

BASIL ROGERS

Following the death of Peter Rogers in August 1923, one of his nephews, Basil Rogers, took over as the groundsman at the St John's College ground. When it came to getting a job as a college groundsman in Oxford, it seems that it was very much a case of 'who you know'. Basil was well trained, however, as his father, Dick Rogers, was a respected cricket groundsman/coach in Bedford.

Basil was a seam bowler and had played for Bedfordshire before and after the First World War, before becoming the professional at Swansea CC. Whilst in South Wales, he also played a couple of first-class matches for Glamorgan in 1923.

Having moved to take the job at St John's College, Basil joined the North Oxford club, which played at the ground. Cricketers often have a favourite team to play against and in Basil's case that team was Banbury. In 1927, he took eight for 31 for North Oxford against Banbury, having already made 86 opening the batting. Even better, in the corresponding fixture in 1931, Basil took all ten wickets! He also turned out intermittently for Oxfordshire from 1925 up until 1935.

Basil was a popular figure at the North Oxford club, especially with the batsmen who played on his excellent pitches. He remained the groundsman at St John's College up until ill health forced him to retire in 1955.

Basil Rogers 1896 - 1975

JOE ROGERS

Whilst Len and Basil were grandsons of Charlie Rogers, remarkably there was also a great-grandson, Joseph 'Joe', who played first-class cricket.

Joe Rogers shared the same name as his grandfather, who was an elder brother of Brusher and Peter. Joe was born in 1908 and as a teenager attracted attention with his big hitting and fiery fast bowling for Cowley St John. He was a small man but could bowl quickly. When only 20 years old, he was selected for Oxfordshire in 1928 and topped the county bowling averages that season with 34 wickets at a cost of just under twelve runs apiece. This led to him being taken on by Gloucestershire in 1929, for whom he made his first-class debut in June of that year against Oxford University, taking a wicket in his first over.

Whilst serving his two-year qualification period for Gloucestershire, Joe made a significant contribution to Oxfordshire's Minor Counties Championship triumph in 1929. In an away game against Bedfordshire that year, he took eight wickets in the host's first innings and another five in the second. Joe finished the season with an impressive haul of 43 wickets for Oxfordshire, at an average of only 12.3.

In May 1930, Joe again played for Gloucestershire against Oxfordshire University in the Parks. Alongside him was a 16-year-old left-arm spinner named Bill Haynes, who was making his first-class debut. Haynes had played a game for Oxfordshire the previous season and was another local lad, having been born in the small village of Cuddesdon, to the east of Oxford. Joe took three early wickets in this match, opening the bowling with Wally Hammond, who went on to score an unbeaten double-century, whilst Bill only bowled three tidy overs.

Joe Rogers played regularly for Gloucestershire in the County Championship in the 1931 and 1932 seasons, but the wickets he took were expensive. He played just a

Oxfordshire's 1929 title winning team.
Back row L-R: Umpire, R Thomas, J Rogers, Scorer, S Lee, E Hartley, Umpire.
Front row L-R: C Walters, L Rogers, B Henry, H Walker, F Hartley.
Sitting: O Claydon, J Arnold.

solitary, final game for Gloucestershire in 1933. That last match was against a Hampshire side that included Arnold, Herman and Brown. Joe claimed his last wicket in first-class cricket when he bowled Johnny Arnold for a duck. Joe and Johnny Arnold were the same age and had grown up together in Cowley, so he would have been pleased with that final wicket.

After finishing with Gloucestershire in 1933, Joe moved back to Oxford and played for Oxford City, as well as a couple more seasons for Oxfordshire. His record in Minor Counties cricket was excellent, but he found it hard stepping up to the first-class game.

At the outbreak of war in 1939, Joe and his wife were living with his parents in Marston. In the 1939 Register, which was a mini census, Joe described himself as a 'cricket professional', so he was still earning a living from the game in some way. He moved to Bath after the war, where he died aged 60.

As for Bill Haynes, having played for Oxfordshire in the early 1930s, he became a regular in Gloucestershire's County Championship side in 1936. As his bowling tailed off, his batting improved, and Bill was given opportunities to open the innings for Gloucestershire. Unfortunately, he struggled to make an impression with either bat or ball and the 1939 season, prior to the outbreak of war, was his last at Gloucestershire. Bill's professional career came to an end at the age of only 25, but with the country once again at war, both he and Joe Rogers had more to worry about than cricket.

Joe Rogers 1908 - 1968
First-class 1929 - 1933 46 matches
45 wickets @ 36.5

Minor Counties Championship 1928 - 1935 34 matches
164 wickets @ 14.6

Neville Rogers – Best of the Family

In August 1934, the former Hampshire stalwart Alec Bowell opened the batting for Oxford City with a 16-year-old lad named Neville Rogers, in a game against the College Servants. They did not know it at the time, but it was the past and future of Hampshire CCC batting combining.

Neville Rogers was Brusher's youngest son. He was born in 1918, making him 21 years younger than his big-hitting brother Len. Due to the age gap, Neville was sometimes mistaken as Len's son, rather than his brother.

Neville stood out for his run-scoring as a schoolboy and was described as being an 'attractive opening batsman' when at Southfield School. He began playing for Oxford City in 1934 and became a consistent run-scorer, noted for his calm temperament.

In 1937, Neville played for South Oxford Boys in the Amos George Cup, which was an under-18s competition. In a game against the Oxford Boys Club, he made a breathtaking score of 170, before retiring! Some disapproving eyebrows were raised at this enormous score, as Neville was then a regular for Oxford City.

Despite making several centuries for Oxford City, Neville was not selected for Oxfordshire, apart from one rain-affected trial game in which he did not bat. Given his family heritage and early promise, it is surprising that he was not given a try by the county.

After leaving school, Neville worked for a meat wholesaler in Oxford. His father, Brusher, died in 1938 but this did not deter him, as he had his heart set on becoming a professional cricketer. In 1939 he went down to Southampton, with hopes of being taken on by Hampshire, together with another young Cowley man named John 'Jack' Godfrey. They played trial games for the Hampshire Club and Ground team that season and both impressed, with Jack making his first-class debut in a Hampshire side that was soundly beaten by the West Indians: but any thoughts of them soon becoming professional cricketers were scuppered by the outbreak of war in September 1939, as they went off to join the army.

Rogers got married during the war and signed as a professional for Hampshire when county cricket resumed in 1946, but by then he was already 28 years old. He made his County Championship debut in May 1946 against Worcestershire, scoring 90 in his first innings, but then failing to score in his next two, he had an inconsistent first season in county cricket. The following year he began opening the batting in partnership with Johnny Arnold and runs began to flow. Both he and Arnold scored over 1,700 runs in County Championship matches that season.

Alan Rayment was a Hampshire team-mate of Arnold and Rogers in the late 1940s, and in 2018, when he was 90 years old, Rayment gave his recollections of these two. Rayment remembered both of them as being top-class. Rogers was a 'cultured' and 'compact' batsman, with a very sound technique. Arnold was more attacking and 'fluent'. Rayment was full of admiration for the batting of both Arnold and Rogers.

Jack Godfrey was also taken on by Hampshire in 1946. He was a seam bowler, but the wickets that he took were not cheap and after a couple of seasons he was released. Jack moved back to Oxford and played for Oxford City and Oxfordshire, before being engaged as a professional by Cambridgeshire.

Meanwhile, Neville Rogers went on to become the mainstay of the Hampshire batting line-up in the immediate post-war period, as a dependable, stylish opening batsman. He was 12th man for England in a Test match against South Africa in 1951, and having scored well over 2,000 runs the following season, was picked to play for the Rest against an England Eleven in a Test Trial in May 1953. He scored an undefeated half-century in this match but could not do enough to gain selection as Len Hutton's opening partner in the England team.

Come the end of the 1955 season, Rogers had a dispute with the Hampshire Committee about the length of a new contract and he decided to retire and go into business. By then he had scored over 15,000 runs for Hampshire in only ten seasons. John Arlott, who was a great admirer of Neville Rogers, wrote fulsomely that, 'His great record since the war ensures him a place amongst the immortals in Hampshire's cricket history.'

'Immortal.' That is praise indeed!

For a couple of seasons after he had retired from Hampshire there were unsuccessful attempts to persuade Neville to play for Oxfordshire. He did return in later years, but only to play more light-hearted matches at the Horspath Feast. As for Jack Godfrey, he came back to local cricket, taking six for 37 as his Pressed Steel team won the Airey Cup final in 1957 and he later played at Horspath.

Neville Rogers.

Neville Rogers was the last of a long line of professional cricketers to come from the small village of Temple Cowley. His childhood home was only a few steps over the road from where George Brown grew up and just around the corner from where Johnny Arnold lived. Before them there had been many other cricket professionals from the village, going back to the time of the Burrin brothers and beyond. It is remarkable that Temple Cowley was a small oasis of cricket for a period of well over a hundred years.

The main reason for Temple Cowley's cricketing heritage was of course its proximity to Cowley Marsh, which became a great breeding ground for local cricketers: but as the University and college teams moved away from Cowley Marsh, so the cricketing heart of Temple Cowley started to beat more slowly and by the 1950s, it was barely a whimper. These days there is just one forlorn-looking artificial wicket on what remains of Cowley Marsh, together with two modern practice nets. No organised cricket is played there anymore.

As for the village of Temple Cowley, it has also been swallowed up into the city of Oxford and its cricketing heritage forgotten, apart from its pub named the Cricketers Arms.

Down in Southampton, with the retirement of Neville Rogers, the 1956 season was the first since 1901 in which there was no Oxford-born player in the Hampshire team: but it would not be long until another Oxford lad named Alan Castell was joining Hampshire.

Neville Rogers 1918 - 2003
First-class 1946 - 1955 298 matches
16,056 runs @ 32.0

Jack Godfrey 1917 – 1995
First-class 1939 - 1947 12 matches
15 wickets @ 50.2

Minor Counties Championship 1939 - 1954 55 matches
53 wickets @ 17.8

No Money in the Game – 1950s and 1960s

English cricket was struggling financially in the 1950s and early 1960s, as income from sponsorship and the BBC's coverage of Test matches was minimal. Attendances at matches were falling and many of the first-class counties were losing money: they could not afford to pay high wages and their professionals would often only be given contracts for one summer at a time.

You would imagine that young, wide-eyed club cricketers would jump at the chance of becoming a professional. Yet some Oxford-born players who emerged at this time took the opposite view when faced with the dilemma of whether to try and make a go of it in the professional game, or to take a better paid, more secure job, and play cricket locally as an amateur, instead.

DAVID LAITT

David Laitt was content to play just Minor Counties cricket, but he could easily have become a professional first-class county cricketer, according to 'Joe' Banton, one of his skippers in the Oxfordshire side. Banton said that Laitt, 'had plenty of offers to turn professional, but there was not the money in the game and David had the stability of a good job. There is no doubt in my mind that he would have made it in the first-class game.'

Two of the counties who showed an interest in Laitt were Northamptonshire and Hampshire, who appreciated his skills close up, when playing Oxfordshire in early season friendlies. But David had a good job at AERE Harwell, before moving into the private sector, and he was not prepared to risk the uncertainty of professional cricket.

Laitt went to Magdalen College School and played for the recently formed Oxfordshire Colts team for two years from 1948, before going off to do his National Service. He played his early club cricket for YMCA and then joined Cowley St John, which had a number of good young cricketers.

From the 1950s onwards, Cowley St John was one of Oxford's dominant clubs, with several county players in the side. Laitt was often the star performer. As an illustration of his mastery, in the 1964 season, David took nine wickets in an innings on three occasions for the 'Jacks'.

Laitt bowled at a brisk medium pace, swinging the ball into the batsman. He could also bowl a leg cutter which according to county team-mate Mike Nurton was basically 'a fast leg break'.

Laitt was first selected for Oxfordshire as a 21-year-old in 1952 and went on to have a prolific 20-year career in Minor Counties cricket, taking what was then a record 670 wickets for Oxfordshire. At times his bowling could be almost unplayable, especially on wet wickets.

Oxfordshire qualified to play in the 60-over Gillette Cup in 1970 and took on Worcestershire in a first-round game in April, at the Morris Motors ground. Wet weather meant that the match had to be played over two days and Worcestershire took 54.5 overs to chase down Oxon's meagre score of 99, thanks to the skilful batting of England players Tom Graveney and Basil D'Oliveira. Bowling against these top batsmen, David Laitt conceded just seven runs off his 12 overs and also picked up a wicket! Unsurprisingly, Graveney was later full of praise for Laitt's bowling.

David went on to be selected for various Minor Counties representative sides. In 1972 he played four matches for Minor Counties South in the 55-over Benson and Hedges Cup and his bowling figures were remarkable in all of these games, especially given the fact that by then he was 41 years old:

v Somerset	11-5-13-2	v Glamorgan	11-5-11-1
v Hampshire	10.2-2-28-3	v Gloucestershire	9.5-3-32-3

These figures show that Laitt could more than hold his

own when bowling against first-class batsmen. David's son Roger remembers a quote from the renowned umpire Dickie Bird, who apparently reckoned that David Laitt was the best bowler that he had seen outside of the professional game.

David Laitt had the ability, but he chose not to turn professional. It seems that he enjoyed being a big fish in a small pond, because according to Mike Nurton, 'He did not suffer fools easily and was intolerant of those who were unable to perform to his own high standards. He enjoyed the limelight and revelled in the acclaim that success brought him'... and wherever he played, David Laitt had a lot of success.

David Laitt 1931 - 1998
First-class 1959 - 1960 2 matches
6 wickets @ 31.0

List A 1967 - 1973 9 matches
14 wickets @ 18.8

Minor Counties Championship 1952 - 1972 139 matches
670 wickets @ 14.9 1,943 runs @ 13.7

TERRY STRANGE
Terry Strange grew up just off the Cowley Road in the 1930s and played cricket for his school on Cowley Marsh. His family home, near the bus depot, was actually built on what in the days of Bancalari and Burrin was part of the then much larger Cowley Marsh. Terry's heritage was very much in the 19th-century cricketing home of Oxford.

Terry was a tall lad and developed into a fast bowler, playing his club cricket for YMCA and the Oxford XIII club. He was first selected for Oxfordshire as a 20-year-old in 1953 and had a long career for the county, restricted by work commitments and National Service, until knee problems forced him to give up the game.

One of his county colleagues described Strange as 'a damn

good bowler', and he was, by his own admission, 'quite quick'. Mike Nurton reckons that Terry was 'definitely good enough to turn professional'.

In 1948, Terry began work at the old John Radcliffe Hospital, before moving to the Nuffield Orthopaedic Hospital, where he had a long career as a rehabilitation engineer. In the early 1950s he was asked to go for a week-long trial at Hampshire but turned the offer down. Terry remembered that in first-class cricket, 'the money was not very good in those days', and professionals had the problem of finding work every winter.

So, Terry was never tempted to leave home in order to play professionally. He was happy to play for Oxfordshire ... when he could get time off work.

Terry Strange 1932 - 2022
Minor Counties Championship 1953 - 1970 41 matches
89 wickets @ 23.6

MIKE NURTON
Mike Nurton had a long career as a teacher, together with a very successful one playing Minor Counties cricket for Oxfordshire, but looking back in his retirement, he considers that it was 'certainly a regret that I did not give it a go' as a professional cricketer.

Nurton's cricketing roots lie just to the west of Oxford, in Boars Hill. From the top of Boars Hill, there is a lovely view of the 'dreaming spires' of Oxford. At the bottom of the hill they have been playing cricket at least since Victorian times and it was at Boars Hill CC that Mike first played cricket as a lad, filling in when his dad's team was a man short.

Nurton showed promise at Abingdon School and was asked to join the Oxford City club, which very conveniently played on the Southern Bypass ground just to the Oxford side of Boars Hill. Living and attending school in Berkshire, he was selected for the under-19 Berkshire Bantams team for three seasons but then declined the offer to play for the full Berkshire side, choosing Oxfordshire instead. From 1963, Nurton went on to play 28 seasons for Oxfordshire, opening the batting and consistently churning out runs, approaching 13,000 of them! Admired by team-mates and respected by opponents, Mike was a nuggety left-handed batsman with a solid technique and he became the backbone of Oxfordshire batting.

Mike batted against some top fast bowlers of the 1970s and 1980s when playing in the Gillette Cup for Oxfordshire or in the Benson and Hedges Cup for Minor Counties representative teams: the West Indians Andy Roberts (Hampshire), Colin Croft (Lancashire) and Joel Garner (Somerset) all tested Nurton's technique and mettle, as did the leading England bowlers Bob Willis (Warwickshire) and Ian Botham (Somerset).

Batting against quick bowling takes some doing for a Minor Counties cricketer. Mike played some gritty innings and won a Man of the Match award for a half-century scored against Lancashire in 1978.

As a schoolboy, Nurton had an unsuccessful trial at The Oval. When playing for Oxfordshire, he was asked whether he would like to go for a trial with Hampshire. Mike declined the offer, taking his father's advice to complete his teacher training at St Luke's College in Exeter, rather than take a risk with the professional game. Teaching could provide a secure, long career, which professional cricket could not.

Mike Nurton has a tinge of regret about never trying to play as a professional but is philosophical about his life in education and cricket. 'I look back with satisfaction and gratitude at having been fortunate to enjoy the best of both worlds. I have had the opportunity of playing with and against many of the best first-class cricketers and at the same time pursuing a career.'

Teaching turned out to be the perfect job for Mike Nurton, as the long summer holidays meant that he could play regularly for his beloved Oxfordshire.

Mike Nurton b 1943
List A 1970 - 1987 27 matches
597 runs @ 27.9

Minor Counties Championship 1963 - 1990 244 matches
12,761 runs @ 33.2

CLIFF HOLTON

Cliff Holton worked in a car factory, playing amateur football as a full back at Oxford City, before signing as a professional for Arsenal in 1947, when only 18 years old. He became a centre forward and played on the losing side in the 1952 FA Cup Final, before winning the league title with Arsenal the following season.

Holton was also an allround cricketer and a particularly fine fielder. After a couple of games for Oxfordshire he played for the second teams at Essex and Middlesex in the 1950s. The stories about him vary, but apparently, he was asked to sign as a professional by Essex or Middlesex, or both, depending on who you believe. He turned these offers down in order to concentrate on his football career, which was a good decision, as he went on to score a phenomenal 293 goals in the Football League for various clubs, before retiring in 1968.

Cliff Holton 1929 - 1996

Alan Castell – Sobers was his Rabbit

There were three spin bowlers in the Hampshire team that played against Somerset at Dean Park, Bournemouth, in July 1963. Two of these, Peter Sainsbury and Alan Wassell, were left-armers, whilst the third was a leg-spinner named Alan Castell, who was just approaching his 20th birthday. Playing a trio of spin bowlers in a County Championship match is almost unheard of now, but it was not unusual for Hampshire to play three spinners that season.

In Somerset's first innings, their batsmen struggled to a score of 156, as Wassell took three wickets and Castell claimed five. Hampshire managed to gain a small first innings lead, but young Castell excelled when Somerset batted again, dismissing most of their top order batsmen to collect another five-wicket haul. Somerset went on to win a close game, but the talk afterwards was about the young spinner Castell, who had the incredible match figures of ten for 102, from 54 overs. The Australian batsman Bill Alley was playing for Somerset in this match and he later suggested that Castell was more promising than Richie Benaud had been at a similar age. Benaud was then the Australian captain and a world class leg-spin bowler, so that was a huge compliment.

In Hampshire's next match, Leicestershire's batsmen collapsed against the seam bowlers and Castell only bowled three overs, but in the following game against Gloucestershire, Castell shone again, taking seven wickets in the match. Had English cricket found a new young star in Alan Castell?

Castell had been born in Oxford during the Second World War. His family lived at 118 Herschel Crescent in Littlemore, in the days before the Oxford Ring Road divided that area off from the rest of the village.

Alan's father, Phil Castell, had played for the local Morris

Motors CC since the late 1930s: he was a middle order batsman and later became club captain, as well as playing some games for the Oxfordshire Club and Ground side.

Having shown his cricketing talent at Northfield School, Alan was selected to play some matches for the Oxfordshire Schoolboys team in August 1957, just after his 14th birthday. He was then considered to be mainly a batsman and opened the batting on his debut against Worcestershire.

Alan began playing club cricket the following season, still aged only 14, although it was not for his father's team, but for the Oxford XIII club. Terry Strange was then one of the senior players at the Oxford XIII club and remembered the young Castell as being 'very talented'.

Alan was selected again for Oxfordshire Schoolboys in 1958. In a match against Buckinghamshire in July, he batted at No 3, but was one of six early wickets to fall, as Oxfordshire struggled to a total of 101. Bowling his leg breaks 'extremely well', according to the *Oxford Times*, Alan then took six for 19, as Buckinghamshire collapsed to 66 all out. Following this success, Alan was nominated for an English Schools trial game and at the end of August played for Southern Schools against the Midlands, at Coventry.

It is a mark of how highly Alan was considered that despite his youth, he was picked to play for the Oxfordshire Colts team in an end of season match against a side containing several county players. They were some good players, as well, for Oxfordshire finished as runners-up to the Yorkshire second team in the Minor Counties Championship that season. It was a great experience for the young lad from Littlemore, albeit that he was bowled for a duck.

Alan must also have impressed when playing in the game at Coventry against Midlands Schoolboys, as he was invited by Warwickshire to go up to their indoor school, the following winter. Tony Bradbury, later to make his name as an Oxford City footballer, accompanied Alan to some of these coaching sessions, where future England batsman

Dennis Amiss was also in attendance.

Come the following summer of 1959, there was a clash of the Castells, when in mid-May, Alan played for Oxford XIII in a match against his dad's Morris Motors team. The Morris men won this encounter, with Phil Castell easily outscoring his son, to maintain his status in the household.

Although only 15 years old, Alan played for both Oxford XIII and Oxford YMCA against many of the top local clubs during the 1959 season. In June, he took a particular liking to the Headington bowlers, scoring a half-century for Oxford XIII as they chased down Headington's score of 241. The following week, under the headline 'Castell's Fine Knock for the YMCA', the *Oxford Times* reported on another defeat for Headington, in which the YMCA openers scored freely and 'A Castell's innings of 75 was particularly noteworthy.'

Still not yet 16, Alan was invited to play for Northamptonshire Second Eleven against Huntingdonshire in July. David Larter, a future England fast bowler, was also playing for the Northants side. 'He was lightening. Heavens above, I had never seen anyone like that before,' remembers Alan. Disconcertingly, one of the Northants opening batsmen was hit by a delivery from Larter in the nets before the game and an ambulance had to be called. Alan fielded amongst some very distant slips to Larter's bowling. Playing with professional cricketers was an eye-opening experience for a raw, young lad, but Alan acquitted himself well with both bat and ball in this match.

After leaving school, Alan was asked to play a few matches for the Warwickshire Club and Ground side. With two first-class counties showing interest in him, it was an exciting time.

In club cricket, Alan was predominantly a batsman but when he was selected for the Oxfordshire Colts later in the season, he was able to display his allround talents. In a game against Suffolk, he took four for 15 with his leg-spinners and then, when the Colts were struggling at 64 for six, he made an undefeated 45 in an unbroken match-winning partnership of 85. All of this, playing two years above his age group.

The final Oxfordshire Colts game of the season was against Hampshire, at the Southampton County Ground, in early September. Alan bowled and batted well, catching the eye of the watching home team coach, Arthur Holt.

Having left school, Alan started working with his father, but both were aware that Warwickshire, Northamptonshire and Hampshire were all showing interest.

'What basically happened was that my dad, bless him, decided that I would go to the first county to offer professional terms. That is when dear old Holty (Arthur Holt, the Hampshire coach) drove all the way to Oxford, despite not being the best driver in the world. I was working with my dad, who was a trimmer by trade in the motor industry. He worked at a place called Cridlands. Arthur Holt came up there and we sat on a bench, and he said to my father, "I want him on the staff. I will look after him, don't worry." So that was more or less it.'

Alan went down to Southampton in the spring of 1960 and Arthur Holt booked him into the YMCA. 'I wasn't very impressed with the YMCA, but it did a job as it was only a brisk walk to the County Ground in Northlands Road. But I had to share a room with two other guys that I had never met in my life.'

Alan made his debut for Hampshire Second Eleven in a match against their Somerset counterparts at Taunton, in May 1960. He took three for 37 in the second innings and altogether played in seven Second Eleven Championship matches that season, with best bowling figures of five for 44 against Kent.

The 1961 season was momentous for Hampshire as the club won the County Championship for the first time, but

Alan did not play in any Championship games, although he made his first-class debut against Oxford University.

It was not until August 1962 that Alan was selected for the Hampshire County Championship side, but initially, his batting impressed more than his bowling. On his debut he helped save the game against Yorkshire by batting out the final overs. Then, when Hampshire met Surrey at Southampton, he came into bat with Hampshire's first innings score at a paltry 128 for eight. Danny Livingstone was batting at the other end and between them they clawed things back, passing the follow-on score and then going on to take the total up to 358, before both were dismissed. By then, Livingstone had made a remarkable double-hundred and Castell scored 76 in a record Hampshire 9th-wicket partnership of 230. That record remains to this day.

Alan started the 1963 season back in the Seconds, but when picked for the first team, he made his dramatic impact in taking ten wickets against Somerset, closely followed by seven against Gloucestershire. But just as he seemed to have the cricketing world at his feet, Castell suddenly had a crisis of confidence and lost control of his leg-spinners. For the last couple of months of the season he struggled to pitch the ball consistently, but despite this, was selected to go on a prestigious International Cavaliers tour to Jamaica in the winter. As an inexperienced 20-year-old, he was amongst a squad full of great names of English cricket, including Ted Dexter, Tom Graveney, Denis Compton, Jim Laker and Fred Trueman. Leg-spinners were a rare species in English cricket in the 1960s, but Alan was joined by another when Robin Hobbs of Essex was added to the squad.

What could have been a great experience for a young county bowler turned out badly for Alan, as he remembers: 'Quite frankly, it was frightening for me, because I had lost all confidence and had a job to let go of the ball. I was absolutely all over the place. Basically, I shouldn't have gone.'

Writing an end of tour report in *The Cricketer*, John Arlott reported that whilst Robin Hobbs had been impressive, 'Unhappily, his fellow leg-spinner, Alan Castell of Hampshire, had a rough time. His experience is of less than a dozen first-class matches, and he had considerable trouble with his length for the second half of the last English season. During this tour, on slow pitches and against batsmen quick to hammer any bad ball, he was never given the chance to settle down. He persevered gamely and with good grace; occasionally he turned both leg-break and googly sharply, but he gained more of sunburn and experience than of confidence.'

Alan returned to life in second team cricket in the 1964 season, one bright spot being the seven wickets that he took in a match against Somerset in early August. He was selected for three first team County Championship games at the end of the season but only picked up a solitary wicket. Alan did not play any first team Championship games the following year and by the middle of the 1966 season, his future with Hampshire was looking very uncertain. Having arrived at the club as an exciting prospect in 1960, six years later it seemed as if his professional career could be ending, at the age of just 23.

Robin Hobbs of Essex was the only English leg-spinner to thrive in this era and he only played seven Test matches for England. According to Alan, leg-spinners 'were considered too high a risk.' With his confidence low and having played the meagre total of just 14 County Championship matches for Hampshire, it appeared that the English game might soon have one fewer leg-spinner.

Derek Shackleton was a consistent seam bowler, who gave batsmen very little. He was dependable and rarely missed a game for Hampshire. Come early July in 1966, something surprising happened: Derek Shackleton was injured and not available to play in the upcoming game against Worcestershire, at the United Services Ground, Portsmouth, which was known for having a quick wicket. The Hampshire selectors needed a seam bowler to replace Shackleton, but it was not obvious where they would find one. Alan takes up the story:

> Leo Harrison, who was the county coach, happened to mention to the county Committee and powers that be, that I had bowled with the new ball in a practice match against the second team on one occasion and they said, well, we will give it a try. They produced a new ball out of the office, which was a record, and I went into the nets. I did not really have a run up. I had a rough idea where to come from and I ran in and banged it in. David Turner was batting in the nets and I bowled him. The Committee stood behind the nets and they made the decision, 'we will give it a whirl' and so I am in the side the next day against Worcester, as a seamer. Jimmy Gray went on before me. I was second change and got six wickets.

As Worcestershire scored 283 for eight declared, Alan had a hand in all of the wickets to fall, taking six for 69 and catching the other two. He could hardly have started his new life as a seam bowler in a more dramatic way. Hampshire batted poorly, but following on, just managed to hold on for a draw.

Alan kept his place in the Hampshire side, generally bowling quite economically and picking up a few wickets, before taking six for 49 in 27 overs against Derbyshire at Southampton. A week later, he took four wickets in Lancashire's first innings. Bowling off a short run, Alan was able to surprise a few batsmen with the pace that he generated.

At the end of August 1966, the West Indians came to play Hampshire. Opening the bowling, Castell took seven wickets in the match, one of them being the legendary Garry Sobers, whom he caught and bowled for 23. The second part of the season had been a success for a reinvented and rejuvenated Alan Castell.

Despite Hampshire's other main seamers doing well, Castell did not prosper over the following couple of seasons.

With the retirement of Derek Shackleton, Alan had more opportunity in 1969 and bowling mostly as first change, found some form. He took six for 22 against Somerset in May and eight wickets in the match against Kent in July, playing in 20 County Championship matches and taking 45 wickets. A highlight of the season was twice bowling Garry Sobers in Hampshire's match against the West Indians. Alan remembers that his captain Roy Marshall would call out, 'Cas, here comes your rabbit,' when Sobers came out to bat against Hampshire.

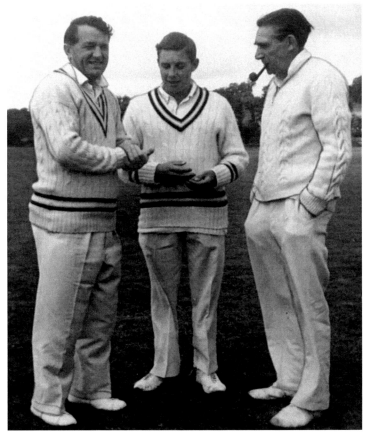

Neville Rogers, Alan Castell and Phil Castell
having a chat at Horspath Feast, early 1960s.

The 40 overs-a-side John Player Sunday League started in 1969 and the following season Castell played a dozen games in this competition, never taking many wickets but only conceding just over four runs an over. Scoring rates were then comparatively low and this was not regarded as particularly economical. More significantly, the 40 wickets that he took in the County Championship that year cost over 41 runs each.

Alan's final year at Hampshire was 1971, with injury causing him to miss the middle of the season. His final wicket for Hampshire came in the last Sunday League game of the season against Sussex, when he bowled former England captain Ted Dexter. A good one to go out on!

Alan's professional career had started with great promise, but faded away and was finished by the time he was 28. He lost his bowling confidence at a young age, something that has happened to others, such as Nasser Hussain, who was an England schoolboy leg-spinner, but then completely 'lost it' and gave up bowling. A lack of opportunity and perhaps a lack of faith by the Hampshire Committee also hindered Castell's development as a wrist-spinner. Alan himself feels that he could have been given more support from the Hampshire management when he was struggling as an inexperienced youngster. Despite the setbacks, he converted himself into a seam bowler, but was never capped by Hampshire, which may be a reflection of his relations with the hierarchy at the club. Alan was a lively, sociable young man of the 1960s and did not always toe the line as the Hampshire management might have wished.

So having started with high expectations, Alan Castell's professional career came to a quiet end, although with some great memories. At Hampshire he played with the imperious Barry Richards and a young Gordon Greenidge. You do not get much better than those two .... apart from Garry Sobers of course!

Another Oxford born player to give it a go in first-class

county cricket in the 1960s was John Martin. A tall, broad-shouldered opening bowler, who went to Magdalen College School, Martin played 17 games for Oxfordshire as a teenager, the last of which was against Somerset Second Eleven in the Minor Counties Championship challenge match in 1961. He took four early Somerset wickets in this game and although Oxfordshire lost, Martin's bowling impressed the west country club.

John then went to Oxford University, playing for the Dark Blues from 1962 to 1965. Whilst a student, after the university term had ended, he also played for the Somerset Second Eleven, as well as a couple of County Championship matches for the first team.

In 1962, the amateur status in English cricket was abolished. Prior to then nearly all Oxbridge cricketers who had gone on to play first-class county cricket did so as amateurs. This was to do with social class, as historically, it was not seen as befitting for a gentleman to besmirch his status by playing as a professional. After 1962, all first-class county cricketers became professional players and Martin was one of the early Oxbridge cricketers to go on to be a professional when he joined the Somerset staff full-time in 1966. Unfortunately, his career at Taunton was very brief, as he could not break into the Somerset Championship side and left the club at the end of that first full season.

Despite failing to impress at Somerset, Martin finished his career with 93 first-class wickets, with a best of seven for 26 in Derbyshire's first innings in the Parks in 1964.

Whilst his seam bowling was good, John's batting is best overlooked, as he had a first-class batting average of under four. He and Alan Castell played against each other a few times, but in their only first-class encounter, Martin was bowled with only two runs to his name, by Hampshire's Castell, when playing for the University in the Parks in 1964. It was probably Alan's easiest ever first-class wicket!

Alan Castell b 1943
First-class 1961 - 1971 112 matches
229 wickets @ 31.0 & 1,622 runs @ 15.9

List A 1966 - 1971 30 matches
28 wickets @ 36.3

John Martin b 1941
First-class 1962 - 1965 40 matches
93 wickets @ 29.0

Minor Counties Championship 1959 - 1972 38 matches
110 wickets @ 20.7

Rupert

Rupert Evans is another Oxford bowler who collected the scalps of world-class West Indian batsmen. When playing for the Minor Counties representative side in matches against the West Indies, he dismissed Desmond Haynes, Richie Richardson and the master, Viv Richards. Although a modest man, if you ask Rupert about how he managed to get Viv Richards out, he will give you a full description with a sparkle in his eyes!

Taking those wickets was special, as Rupert hails from the Caribbean, having been born in Kingston, Jamaica in February 1954. Lawrence Rowe, a future star West Indies batsman, went to Rupert's school, a few years ahead of him. Sport was of a high standard at his school, but the only cricket that Rupert played in Jamaica was with his friends.

In 1967, when he was 13 years old, Rupert and his sister came over to join his parents, who were living in Sparkhill, Birmingham. Two years later, the family moved down to Oxford, where Rupert attended the Cowley St John school. He was spotted on a visit to the school by Paul Collins, an Oxford Willows player, and was asked to join the club. Derek Primett, the Willows captain, encouraged young players and although very inexperienced, Rupert was selected for Oxfordshire Under-15s, after impressing at trials. He soon progressed up to the Oxfordshire Colts side, where he not only bowled off spin, but also went on to open the batting.

It is ironic that Rupert had very little opportunity to play cricket up until he was 15 years old, because later in life he would work hard to give the youngsters of Oxfordshire the chance to play cricket from a young age.

Rupert joined his local Cowley St John club in 1973 and that year, whilst still playing for Oxfordshire Colts, was selected for the full county side. He would go on to captain both club and county. With Rupert bowling his economical off spin and also sometimes opening the batting, Cowley St John won the Cherwell League and Oxfordshire Knock Out Cup many times. He was also in the Oxfordshire sides that won the Minor Counties Championship in 1974, 1982 and 1989. In that era, unlike most other sides, Oxfordshire never used professionals and most team members played club cricket locally. Oxfordshire had some good cricketers and Rupert Evans was one of the best: but playing a full season of Minor Counties cricket was sometimes a problem for Rupert, as he worked at Oxford University Press and getting time off could be difficult.

Rupert spent one successful season playing for Walsall in the Birmingham League, but his commitments as the county captain curtailed this. He went on to be selected for the Minor Counties representative side, playing in the Benson and Hedges Cup and against many touring international teams, as well as for the England Amateur Eleven.

In a Benson and Hedges match in 1988 for the Minor Counties against Northamptonshire, despite not taking a wicket, only scoring three not out and being on the losing side, Rupert won the Man of the Match award. He bowled 11 overs in that match, conceding just 21 runs, against a Northants side whose top five in the batting order had all played, or would play, for England.

The only first-class match that Rupert played was for the Minor Counties against the touring Indians in 1990. He dismissed both Ravi Shastri and Kapil Dev in this game, although not before they had scored plenty of runs.

Rupert went on a number of overseas tours, including a trip with the Club Cricket Conference in 1989 to the Caribbean, although there were no games in Jamaica. He also toured South Africa with the Minor Counties side in 1994. Although the apartheid regime had been overturned by then, Rupert had reservations and initially declined the invitation, before being persuaded to go. With security concerns and as the only black man in the squad, playing mostly all white sides, it was an experience, but the quality of the cricket was high.

Towards the end of his playing days, at the age of 53, Rupert bowled with typical consistency, as Oxford CC won the Home Counties Premier League in 2007, adding to his vast collection of winners medals.

Any cricketer that you speak to who batted against Rupert Evans will tell you the same thing. There were no easy runs to be scored when Rupert was bowling. His off spin was always probing, always on the spot.

Rupert played nearly all of his cricket as an amateur, but some think that he could have become a professional. Tim Hancock, the Gloucestershire batsman, played with Rupert for Oxfordshire prior to turning professional. Recalling his time with Oxfordshire, Hancock told the *Oxford Times*, 'I played with some good players. Rupert Evans would have made it as a county cricketer, easily.' Rupert did have a trial for Northamptonshire, but nothing came of that. In middle age, however, he started to earn a living out of cricket.

In 1996, the ECB came up with a plan to employ a Cricket Development Officer in each county and Rupert was appointed to this role in Oxfordshire. From Kwik Cricket upwards, Rupert strove to develop the game in the county, working as a one-man band for 18 years. He did a very good job and was instrumental in setting up a new partnership with Sussex CCC in 2013, which has worked well for both counties.

Rupert has always done a lot of coaching and he became the Oxfordshire Head Coach, overseeing Oxfordshire's National Counties Championship win in 2021 and the National Counties Twenty20 triumph in 2022.

Although he never turned professional as a player, Rupert's passion and knowledge of the game has led him to a working career in cricket later in life, developing and coaching the game. He could write an interesting book about his cricketing career, having played all around England and in many countries around the world, although unfortunately, never in Jamaica.

In Oxfordshire cricketing circles, you do not need to say his surname, because just about everyone seems to know Rupert. Through playing, coaching and his work promoting the game, Rupert Evans is well known, and more importantly, very well respected.

Rupert Evans b 1954
List A 1983 - 1986 28 matches
13 wickets @ 72.5

Minor Counties Championship 1973 - 1998 157 matches
451 wickets @ 25.9

Dave Ligertwood – Oxford's Aussie

'I love Oxford', is Dave Ligertwood's opinion of the city of his birth. Despite living in Australia nearly all of his life, he clearly still has a strong attachment to Oxford.

Dave's parents came over from Adelaide so that his father, Andrew, could do a postgraduate degree at Oxford University. During their stay, Dave was born in 1969, before the family moved back to Australia.

Andrew became a university lecturer in Adelaide, but the family liked Oxford so much that every four years or so, when he was able to take study leave, they would return. On one nine-month trip to Oxford in 1984, Dave attended Magdalen College School and also played for Oxfordshire Under-15s. Four years later, he returned on a school tour to England and featured in a double-century opening partnership in a match against Magdalen College School.

Dave was a batsman with a good technique, but also took up wicketkeeping when he was 17. He went on to be selected for the Australian Universities side and then progressed into the South Australia Second Eleven.

Nasser Hussain came over to play for Dave's club in Adelaide and it was Nasser who suggested to him that with his British birth, he could play county cricket. Throughout the 1990s, during the Australian winter, Dave would come over to England to play cricket. In 1990, he turned out for Hertfordshire, as he did the following year, when he also had several matches for Surrey Second Eleven. He was taken on at The Oval for the 1992 season and with Alec Stewart going away to play for England, was picked as wicketkeeper and also opening batsman in four County Championship matches. Unfortunately, Dave failed to score many runs and Surrey released him at the end of the season, telling him that his wicketkeeping needed more work. Dave recalls that this was 'pretty shattering' but it strengthened his resolve to work harder in the future.

Coming back to England in 1994, Dave played second eleven cricket at Worcestershire, Essex and Durham. Liking what they saw, Durham recruited Dave and he played there for three seasons up until 1997. Some of his best performances for Durham came when playing against his old club Surrey.

After his playing days, Dave has continued to work in the world of cricket, with considerable success. He set up a sports agency which represented some top cricketers and had offices in England, Australia and India. In the early years of the Indian Premier League, he worked with Lalit Modi to source many overseas players. Dave then sold that business and in 2012 was the co-founder, with Bronte Eckerman, of a new company called Zing International, which has been responsible for lighting up the game of cricket over the last few years.

Bronte Eckerman had come up with the idea of bails which would flash when the wicket was broken, and he joined forces with Dave Ligertwood to develop and market these bails. Dave took the idea to the television companies and governing bodies, which showed enthusiasm, and their flashing Zing bails are now seen in cricket matches all over the world. The flashing bails have the benefit of showing the exact moment the wicket is broken, helping both the crowd and also the third umpire on television replays, as well as adding some drama. As Dave says, 'It has been a good little success story.'

The system has been developed so that the stumps also flash as soon as a bail is removed, further adding to the spectacle. Dave Ligertwood had a good eye for a cricket ball, and as technology has come more and more into top level cricket, he also recognised a good invention when he saw one.

David Ligertwood b 1969
First-class 1992 - 1996 28 matches
733 runs @16.7 80 dismissals (71 ct 9 st)

List A 1991 - 1996 32 matches
373 runs @ 20.7 38 dismissals (31 ct 7st)

All Change

Club cricket seemed to be prospering in Oxford, and indeed Oxfordshire, in the 1980s and this was reflected by the county winning the Minor Counties Championship twice in that decade, using almost exclusively local players.

All was not well with the leading clubs in the city, however, and there would be a lot of change in the years leading up to the turn of the millennium and just after. The quality and abundance of college cricket grounds had been a long-time strength of Oxford cricket, but the reliance on college grounds would eventually prove to be the downfall of some of its larger clubs.

In 1993, North Oxford, Headington, Cowley St John and Pressed Steel were fighting it out in Division One of the Cherwell League, but within a few years all of these old-established clubs went out of existence. In 1994, the Cowley St John and Headington clubs merged to form a new Oxford CC. Two years later, a new Bicester and North Oxford club began playing at a ground in Chesterton, near Bicester, following the merger of the two previously independent clubs.

Come 2001, another merger saw a new Oxford and Horspath club begin playing at the village ground, but this amalgamation only lasted three seasons before a split back into the original two clubs. Meanwhile, the Pressed Steel club had changed its name to Rover Cowley in 1995, but was then taken over by Oxford CC.

So in the space of 11 years the city had lost its four top clubs and gained a new Oxford CC. Cowley St John and North Oxford had always played on college grounds and for decades this worked well, although there had been the perennial drawback of shared use. The problem was that come the 1990s, with league cricket firmly established, youth cricket developing and third and fourth teams having to be accommodated, clubs needed to expand, but this was just not possible when using a single college ground.

Bicester and North Oxford's large new ground, with good practice facilities, a bar to provide income, and unrestricted access was just what was needed. In the case of Headington, its ground had been created when it moved from the Manor Ground, but from the outset it had been too small. There was literally not enough space to grow the club. A plan was hatched to merge with Cowley St John, sell the Barton Road site for housing and build a new ground. Unfortunately, the latter part of the plan was scuppered by the planners!

All of these mergers reduced the amount of cricket being played in Oxford and the opportunity for talented youngsters to play club cricket of a good standard in the city was greatly diminished. But as cricket in Oxford was contracting, so the fortunes of some village clubs around the city improved, as teams such as Horspath, Tiddington and Cumnor all prospered. It would be these village clubs, together with Abingdon Vale, that would go on to provide stepping stones for some new professional cricketers from the Oxford area.

There was another change in 2000, when an elite Home Counties league was created. By 2023, Cumnor and Horspath were playing alongside Oxford in Division Two of this league, whilst Tiddington was in Division One of the Cherwell League, together with Bicester and North Oxford.

Change was also taking place at Oxford University. With playing standards at the University having declined over the previous couple of decades, it merged with Oxford Brookes University in 2000, to form one of eight university centres of excellence.

These days, Oxford University has lost its first-class status. The last three-day Varsity match to be played at Lord's took place in 2000, as the fixture at HQ became a one-day game after that. However, the *Holding Up a Mirror to Cricket* report recommended to MCC that as the game of cricket strives to be more inclusive, this match should no longer be played at Lord's after 2023. The elite privileged position that Oxford University held in English cricket since 1827 has now disappeared and as the game strives for more equality of opportunity, regardless of where anyone is educated, that cannot be seen as a bad development.

The decline in Oxford University cricket means that it is unlikely that any great cricketers will ever again be seen in the Parks. The last time that there was anything like a stir when a star player came to Oxford was in 2015, when Kevin Pietersen scored 170 for Surrey against Oxford MCCU in the Parks, as he was seeking to get back into the England team. Pietersen never did regain his place in the England side and cricket at Oxford University is unlikely to make a comeback either.

Gloucestershire Connection

Around the turn of the millennium, Gloucestershire became a formidable side in limited-overs cricket. They had no big-name overseas players or any great top order batsmen, but what they did have was a team with a clear understanding of the one-day game and how they would go about playing it.

Gloucestershire would pressurise the opposition batsmen. Wicketkeeper Jack Russell had the ability to stand up to the wicket when the left-arm seamer Mike Smith opened the bowling. Australian seam bowler Ian Harvey became a master of the disguised slower ball and bowling at the end of an innings. Their spinners would hurry through their overs. They also put an emphasis on fitness and fielding. In this way, Gloucestershire became a force in one-day cricket.

Two batsmen with a connection to Oxford, and Oxfordshire, were involved in Gloucestershire's rise to prominence. These two were Tim Hancock and Rob Cunliffe, who had played together for Oxfordshire Colts, and both also had some games for Oxfordshire before becoming professionals at Gloucestershire.

Both of them contributed to Gloucestershire's success in 1999, when Yorkshire was beaten by a wide margin in the final of the Benson and Hedges Super Cup at Lord's. Opener Tim Hancock (35) and No 3 Rob Cunliffe (61) ably supported centurion Mark Alleyne, as they rattled up 291 for nine in their 50 overs, which proved way too much for Yorkshire. Four weeks later, Gloucestershire returned to Lord's, beating Somerset to win the National Westminster Bank Trophy, with opener Hancock (74) top scoring, although Cunliffe only made a few runs.

In the following season of 2000, Gloucestershire won all three limited-overs trophies. Tim Hancock (60) again top scored for Gloucestershire, and Rob Cunliffe (24) contributed, as Glamorgan's total was successfully chased down in the final of the Benson and Hedges Cup. Both played in Gloucestershire's Sunday League-winning side, but only Hancock was in the team that beat Warwickshire in the final of the National Westminster Trophy. Five trophies in two seasons was an amazing achievement for the men from Bristol. It did not stop there, as Gloucestershire won the Cheltenham and Gloucester Trophy in 2003 and 2004, with Hancock playing in the latter final, although he was not needed to bat.

As a teenager, Oxford-born Rob Cunliffe was selected for Oxfordshire Colts whilst playing club cricket for Banbury Twenty. His batting talent shone through, and he rose to prominence in 1993, playing six England Under-19 Test matches against India and West Indies, in which he batted exceedingly well, averaging an impressive 58. Rob also made some appearances for Oxfordshire and signed for Gloucestershire, where he went on to play first-class cricket from 1994 until 2001. Hampered by injury, family illness and inconsistency, he never became established in the County Championship side and was considered to be more of a limited-overs batsman. Rob moved on to Leicestershire, where he played for a couple more seasons before retiring from the pro game, although he then had the odd game for Oxfordshire.

Tim Hancock is slightly older than Rob Cunliffe, having been born in Reading in 1972. He went to St Edward's School in Oxford and played for Oxfordshire Colts, as well as some club cricket at Headington. In 1990, he had seven uneventful games for Oxfordshire as an 18-year-old, but impressed in a Gloucestershire trial game in Cheltenham and was signed by the county the following year. Hancock went on to play 15 seasons for Gloucestershire and subsequently has had a number of coaching jobs, including Head of Performance at the Gloucestershire Cricket Board and then Head of Talent Pathway at Gloucestershire CCC.

In the late 1990s, Hancock and Cunliffe were joined on

the Gloucestershire staff by Oxford-born fast bowler Ben Gannon. Ben made an impression in his debut County Championship match in 1999, taking six for 80 in Glamorgan's first innings. He had a promising first season in the Championship but could not force his way into the successful limited-overs side. Held back by injury, Ben played another three seasons at Gloucestershire, before signing for Middlesex in 2003, where he became a team-mate of Andrew Strauss. Gannon and Strauss had previously played together for Oxfordshire Colts, when the future England captain was a Radley College schoolboy. Whilst Strauss went on to great things, Gannon only ever played one season at Middlesex.

In the younger days of Cunliffe, Hancock and Gannon, in the late 1980s and early 1990s, there was no pathway from playing cricket in Oxfordshire to joining a first-class county. But in the new millennium, Oxfordshire entered into a partnership with Gloucestershire, whereby talented young players could join the Gloucestershire Academy. Out of this arrangement, Jack Taylor, from the strong Great Tew club in the north of Oxfordshire, went on to sign for Gloucestershire. It was Taylor who brought some one-day success back to the West Country when he put in a Man of the Match performance as Gloucestershire beat Surrey in the 2015 final of the Royal London One-Day Cup. Younger brother Matty Taylor also went on to join Gloucestershire.

The Oxfordshire/Gloucestershire partnership ended over ten years ago, but it contributed to the westward flow of cricketers from Oxford in recent years, as Miles Hammond, Ben and Luke Charlesworth, and also Tom and Ollie Price, have all joined up with the Taylor brothers on the Gloucestershire staff.

Long ago, there was another significant move between the two counties. Many generations of the Grace family had lived in the village of Charlbury, which lies fifteen miles to the north-west of Oxford. One adventurous young man of the family decided to leave home in Charlbury and moved to near Bristol. That man later had a grandson, named William Gilbert Grace, who became the most famous cricketer in the land and along with his brothers, made Gloucestershire a cricketing stronghold.

Tim Hancock b 1972
First-class 1991 - 2005 185 matches
8,485 runs @ 28.2 47 wickets @ 38.6

List A 1991 - 2005 211 matches
4,153 runs @ 22.2 47 wickets @ 24.8

Rob Cunliffe b 1973
First-class 1994 - 2003 68 matches
2,542 runs @ 23.8

List A 1993 - 2003 92 matches
1,984 runs @ 27.2

Ben Gannon b 1975
First-class 1999 - 2003 32 matches
85 wickets @ 33.3

Born but not Bred

There are a couple of cricketers, of different generations, who were born in the Oxford area, but moved away at a very young age. The medics of Oxford helped to bring them into this world, but otherwise the city had no influence on their lives or cricketing careers.

EDMUND 'NED' ECKERSLEY
'Ned' Eckersley was born in Oxford in 1989. His father, James, was an orthopaedic specialist who worked in Oxford hospitals in the late 1980s and early 1990s.

The family moved to London and Ned went to school in Ealing, where he later joined the strong local cricket club. As a batsman who could also keep wicket, he joined Leicestershire in 2011 and had a superb season in 2013, when he averaged 50, batting at No 3. The highlight for him that year was scoring centuries in both innings in a game against Worcestershire. He went one better in 2016, when he made centuries in three successive innings.

In 2019, Ned moved to Durham and captained the club the following Covid-19-hit year, as well as keeping wicket. He scored well for Durham, apart from in his final season for the club in 2022, after which he retired from first-class cricket.

Ned has played a few times in Oxford. In his younger days at Ealing, he came down the M40 to play a couple of cup games against Oxford CC and whilst at Leicestershire he played two warm-up matches against Oxford MCCU in the Parks. Both of the games were in March, however, so warm-up is perhaps not the correct description, for the Parks is so open that three sweaters are sometimes needed to keep off the chill in early season.

Edmund 'Ned' Eckersley b 1989
First-class 2011 - 2022 147 matches
7,314 runs @ 31.5 275 dismissals (270 ct 5 st)

List A 2008 - 2021 46 matches
1,091 runs @ 29.5

Twenty20 2012 - 2022 92 matches
1,061 runs @ 18.0

PETER ROEBUCK

Peter Roebuck was born in the small village of Oddington, to the north of Oxford, in 1956. His father Jim had come down from the north to study for a degree in Oxford, but the family moved away when Peter was only three years old.

Roebuck was offered a place at both Oxford and Cambridge Universities to study law, but he chose Cambridge, as Oxford apparently showed little interest in his cricketing ability. A diligent batsman, Roebuck played well for Cambridge University, before having a long professional career at Somerset from 1974 to 1991. He scored consistently for Somerset, notching up seven centuries in the 1984 season. England tried out a large number of batsmen in the 1980s, but Roebuck was unfortunate not to be one of them.

As captain of Somerset, Roebuck bore the brunt of the local fury at the decision to release Viv Richards and Joel Garner from the club in 1986, which also led to Ian Botham leaving.

After retiring from first-class cricket, Roebuck played for Devon and had considerable success as a bowler when coming up against Oxfordshire. His most impressive bowling performance was at the Pressed Steel ground in July 1994, when he took nine for 12, as the county of his birth was bowled out for just 40.

Roebuck emigrated to Australia after his playing days were over. He soon established himself as a successful cricket journalist down under, both in print and on television and radio. A complicated character, Roebuck led a sometimes-controversial life, which ended in very sad circumstances when he committed suicide in South Africa in 2011.

Peter Roebuck 1956 - 2011
First-class 1974 - 1991 355 matches
17,558 runs @ 37.3 72 wickets @ 49.2

List A 1975 - 2001 98 matches
7,244 runs @ 29.8 51 wickets @25.1

Jack Brooks – Headband, Headingley and Heart

There is a red and blue England Lions shirt printed with the name BROOKS, hanging on the back wall of the Tiddington CC clubhouse. This shirt was worn by Jack Brooks, who began playing for the Tiddington third team as a youth and went on to climb nearly to the top of the cricketing ladder.

Brooks was a late starter in professional cricket, as he was 25 years old when he made his first-class debut for Northamptonshire against the Australians, in 2009. He quickly progressed up the rungs after that, as over the following six years his attacking fast bowling earned him selection for the England Lions and he won two County Championship winners medals with Yorkshire.

Although born in Oxford, Jack Brooks lived in the village of Tiddington, where there is a successful, close knit cricket club, which in 1995 played at Lord's in the final of the National Village Cup. Jack was only an 11-year-old whippersnapper then. Growing up, he went to Wheatley Park School, but his cricketing education was very much at Tiddington, where he went on to establish a reputation with his fast bowling.

Moving up a level, Brooks played three seasons for Oxford CC, putting in some dynamic bowling performances when the club won the Home Counties League in 2007. Jack only began playing regularly for Oxfordshire in 2008 and after a few second-team games at Surrey and Northamptonshire that season, finally became a professional cricketer when he joined Northamptonshire in 2009, at the age of 24. He established himself as a regular in the Northants side in 2010, playing in all formats, and after continuing to impress, moved up to Yorkshire in 2013. He went on to have success, taking 71 first-class wickets as the Tykes won the County Championship in 2014 and then 69 wickets when they won the title again the following season, bowling particularly well at the Headingley ground.

England had come calling when Jack was selected for the Lions tour to Bangladesh and Sri Lanka in early 2012. He played alongside the youthful Root, Bairstow, Roy, Buttler, Woakes and Hales in some competitive 50-over games on that trip. Following his impressive bowling for Yorkshire, Brooks again played for England Lions on a tour to South Africa in early 2015, where in a game against South Africa A he opened the bowling with Mark Wood and scored an undefeated half-century.

There is a touch of the showman about Jack Brooks: wearing a distinctive headband, he likes to be noticed. Yorkshire folk have a reputation for being dour and hard to please, but they appreciated Jack. *The Yorkshire Post* credited him with adding 'more than a dash of charismatic colour' to their side and being 'a little bit mad in the nicest sense of the word': but what they most liked about him at Yorkshire was the 316 first-class wickets that he took, in his six seasons at the club. A wholehearted cricketer, Jack Brooks has been a popular character wherever he has played. In his final match for Yorkshire, against Worcestershire at the end of the 2018 season, he signed off flamboyantly, taking six first-innings wickets and then biffing 83 when batting at No 10.

The shine of Yorkshire's success was wiped away by the fallout from the testimony of racism given by former player, Azeem Rafiq, about some players, coaching staff and the club as a whole. As Yorkshire CCC subsequently disintegrated, some of Brooks' former team-mates were sanctioned by the ECB. Jack himself was reprimanded for using racially offensive terms in tweets to cricketing friends Tymal Mills and Stewart Laudat, and he also apologised to Cheteshwar Pujara for giving him an anglicised nickname when he played at Yorkshire. After the Yorkshire morass came the *Holding Up a Mirror to Cricket* report in 2023, which forcibly made the point that cricket is a game for all

Jack Brooks bowling for Yorkshire against Durham at Scarborough, 2013.

and everyone should be respected.

Brooks moved to Somerset in 2019, helping the west country club to the runners-up spot in the County Championship in his first season. As opportunities to play in the Somerset side diminished, Jack had a brief spell on loan at Sussex in 2022, where he took his 500th first-class wicket when he dismissed Billy Root in a match against Glamorgan. He had further loan spells at Worcestershire and Nottinghamshire in 2023, before returning to finish his career at Somerset.

The cricket shirt on display in the Tiddington clubhouse is a tribute to an enthusiastic, lion-hearted cricketer. It also reflects well on the village club that set him off on his career in cricket.

Jack Brooks b 1984
First-class 2009 - 2023   154 matches
531 wickets @ 27.7   2,103 runs @ 16.7

List A 2009 - 2023   51 matches
58 wickets @ 33.5   152 runs @ 9.5

Twenty20 2010 - 2023   76 matches
72 wickets @ 25.7   77 runs @ 12.8

From Cumnor to China, Canada and Cape Town

The village of Cumnor is located at the top of a steep hill, to the west of Oxford. They have been playing cricket in Cumnor for a long time. Going all the way back to 1767, it was reported that 11 men from the village played a match at Longworth against a team of Lord Ashbrook's Servants, for the sizeable stake of one and a half guineas and half a penny a man.

Today, Cumnor has a thriving club and three cricketers who played there as youngsters have gone on to be professional cricketers, travelling across the world to play in such places as China, Canada and Cape Town.

Nineteen-year-old fast bowler Simon Cook took 50 wickets for Cumnor when the club won Division Three of the Cherwell League in 1996. Towards the end of the season, he was spotted by Middlesex scout Ian Gould, who had come to cast an eye over Andrew Strauss in an Oxfordshire Colts game. Cook was taken on at Middlesex the following year, but having made such a huge leap, it took a while until he broke into the first team in 1999. Unfortunately, injury then held him back, but he came to the fore in the National League in 2004, equalling the competition record by taking 39 wickets that season.

Cook moved to Kent the following year and was in the team that won the Twenty20 Cup in 2007. In the frenzy of the final against Gloucestershire he had the most economical bowling figures on either side, taking one for 16 off four overs, as Kent won the trophy with three balls to spare.

When he retired from playing in 2012, Simon had to work his way up from the bottom, in the world of coaching. Initially he did some in France, before taking various roles in Hong Kong, of which he had some previous knowledge, having been on an MCC tour to China and Hong Kong as a player. Simon then returned home to become the bowling coach at Kent in 2019, before being appointed Director of Cricket in 2023. His cricketing career has taken him from Cumnor to Canterbury, passing through China on the way.

George Munsey is another former Cumnor cricketer who has ventured around the world, but his most memorable game was not too far away. In 2018 he played in a one-day international between Scotland and England in Edinburgh, finishing on the winning side: but having been born in Oxford and come from the heart of England, in that match Munsey wore the blue shirt of the Scottish Bravehearts.

Going back a while, Tony Munsey played at Cumnor and he took his young son George along to the club. As a young boy, left-handed batsman George stood out when playing Kwik Cricket for the power and timing with which he hit the ball. He attended the Dragon Prep School in Oxford and played for the Oxfordshire Under-10s. Golf then became a priority, a game at which with his natural timing, he excelled.

At the age of 13, George headed up to Scotland, when he began a golf scholarship at the Loretto School, to the east of Edinburgh. Although concentrating on golf, he still played cricket at school and went on to join the Grange CC in Edinburgh. Through residence he qualified to play cricket for Scotland and he worked his way up through the Scottish Development side and Scotland A, before making his debut for the full Scotland team in 2014. Having moved to Scotland with thoughts of becoming a golfer, he had ended up as a professional cricketer!

Skip forward four years to 2018 and as an established member of the Scotland team George found himself playing in a one-day international against England. There was a full house at the Edinburgh ground for that match and most of the spectators went home very happy, having seen a remarkable Scottish victory.

In limited-overs matches, a fantastic performance from

one player can be decisive and it was Calum MacLeod's undefeated 140 in 94 balls that made the difference that day. A century partnership between MacLeod and Munsey helped Scotland to the mighty total of 371 for five in 50 overs. Although missing Stokes and Buttler, a strong England batting line up chased hard, but needing seven runs to win off as many balls, last man Mark Wood was out lbw and Scotland had won. After that defeat, England had a tremendous run in one-day international cricket, which culminated in winning the World Cup in 2019.

Batting at No 5 in that match, George Munsey scored 55 at better than a run a ball. Not afraid to use the reverse sweep, he batted fluently and held his nerve, to help Scotland to a glorious victory.

Twenty20 cricket has been Munsey's forte. An example of his striking power came in a Twenty20 game for Scotland against Holland in 2019, when he scored 127 not out in just 56 balls. He hit 14 sixes in this innings of unbridled severity. George went on to play in the 2021 Twenty20 World Cup, which was disappointing for Scotland, but he had another very memorable day at the Twenty20 World Cup the following year in Australia. In a group game against the West Indies, George opened the batting and scored an undefeated 66. The West Indies batsmen then crumbled as Scotland pulled off a shock win. George won the Man of the Match award in that game, but disappointingly Scotland then lost to Ireland and Zimbabwe and failed to qualify for the next stage.

George Munsey is very much a modern cricketer in that he is a white ball specialist, who plays where opportunities arise. He has had more clubs than in his golf bag, having turned out in in a few Twenty20 and 50-over matches for Leicestershire, Hampshire and Kent, as well as playing overseas franchise cricket in such diverse places as Canada, United Arab Emirates and Hong Kong. His natural aggressive batting makes him an ideal white ball cricketer and in concentrating on that format, he has hardly played any first-class cricket since he first appeared for Northamptonshire against the Australians in 2015.

George returned to his boyhood home in 2016 when he played club cricket for Oxford CC in the Home Counties League, as well as having three games for Oxfordshire: that was just one of his brief ventures south, as he is now firmly established north of the border, looking to help Scotland to further success.

In 2010, when George Munsey returned from Scotland during the summer school holiday, he played for Cumnor alongside Miles Hammond, a promising 14-year-old lad. Hammond was highly thought of, already having played a game for Gloucestershire Second Eleven earlier that season.

Although born in Cheltenham, Hammond had lived in Oxford from a young age, playing at St Edward's School and then for Cumnor in the Cherwell League. A right-arm off-spin bowler and left-handed batsman, Miles played for Oxfordshire age group sides before joining the Gloucestershire Academy. At that time, he was considered to be primarily a bowler and he made rapid progress. Miles was selected for an England Under-19 tour to South Africa in 2013, making his Under-19 Test match debut at Cape Town just after passing his 17th birthday. It had been a very swift rise from playing cricket at the top of the hill in Cumnor to beside the Table Mountain in Cape Town.

Hammond also made his first-class debut for Gloucestershire later in 2013, in a match against Glamorgan, but this was a chastening experience: he failed to score in his only innings and had match bowling figures of one for 156.

After leaving school, Hammond joined Gloucestershire full-time, but his bowling became erratic. Whilst he described it as 'not full-on yips' he found it hard to pitch the ball consistently. Perhaps it was a build-up of pressure due to the intensity of top-class cricket. Whatever the reason, he had to work on his batting in order to extend his career. It took a while, but the breakthrough came when Miles scored a century when opening the innings against Sussex, in July 2018, in what was only his fourth County Championship match. Against a strong bowling attack that included Jofra Archer, he showed that he had the quality to be a top-order batsman.

Looking back on his travails in converting from a bowler into a batsman, Miles has seen it as a positive experience overall, particularly as it is very much a batsman's game in white ball cricket.

Hammond has developed into a forceful batsman and his attacking, risk-taking instincts have brought him success in Twenty20 cricket for Gloucestershire. Miles was signed to play for Birmingham Phoenix when the new Hundred competition was launched in 2021 and some impressive performances in the Phoenix orange shirt led to him being retained in following years. There should be plenty more runs to come from the bat of Miles Hammond in future years ... but it is unlikely that he will be taking many more wickets.

Simon Cook b 1977
First-class 1999 - 2012 141 matches
342 wickets @ 32.1 2,577 runs @ 16.6

List A 1997 - 2012 190 matches
234 wickets @ 27.9 1,253 runs @ 16.9

T20 2003 - 2012 73 matches
85 wickets @ 22.6 168 runs @ 18.7

George Munsey b 1993

Miles Hammond b 1996

Abingdon's Helping Hand

The cricket ground at Abingdon Vale CC has pretty views, looking towards the River Thames, although the pavilion is a less pleasing sight. Going back a decade or so, it was the young cricketers at the club that were catching the eye, rather than any of the scenery.

In 2010, allrounder Graham Charlesworth joined Abingdon Vale as a player and youth coach. Graham was a former first-class cricketer who had become the Head Coach at Oxford University. Amongst the youngsters that he coached at Abingdon were his two sons, Ben and Luke, together with Harrison Ward, another local lad. With Abingdon Vale gaining a reputation for promoting youth cricket, Tom and Ollie Price, who lived to the west of Oxford, came over to join. Remarkably, all five of these Oxford-born youngsters have gone on to be professional cricketers, with the two sets of brothers joining Gloucestershire and Harrison Ward being recruited by Sussex.

The young lads all played in Abingdon Vale's successful age group sides, before Harrison Ward moved on to Horspath. Ben Charlesworth and Tom Price were soon given opportunities to play club cricket at a young age for Abingdon Vale in Division Two of the Cherwell League. Tom Price first played for Abingdon Vale at the age of 12 and was opening the batting for the first team when only 14 years old: he was a small lad and only used as an occasional bowler, but according to club veteran spinner Paul White, even then had a 'golden arm', with the ability to take a wicket or two. Ollie Price was then the next youngster to be blooded in the men's teams. Playing age group cricket for Oxfordshire, both sets of brothers were brought into the Gloucestershire youth coaching system and subsequently moved on from Abingdon to other clubs, in order to play league cricket of a higher standard.

Left-handed batsmen Ben Charlesworth and Harrison Ward were both selected to play for England Under-19s against South Africa in 2018. Ben went on to have a successful career at this level, scoring an impressive 82 against Australia in the 2020 Under-19 World Cup, before a broken knuckle ended his tournament.

Ben Charlesworth made his first-class debut for Gloucestershire in 2018, followed two years later by Tom Price, who by then was primarily a seam bowler. Off-spinning allrounder Ollie Price then made his first-class debut in 2021, whilst seam bowler Luke Charlesworth signed a three-year rookie contract with Gloucestershire a year later, before making his first-class debut in September 2023.

Tom Price bowled impressively towards the end of the 2022 season and started off with a bang the following year when he scored a century when batting at No 9 in a County Championship game against Worcestershire. Later in the day, he then took a hat-trick! Younger brother Ollie also made his mark in the 2023 season, scoring heavily in the Metro Bank One-Day Cup.

Ollie Price.

Having moved to Horspath, Harrison Ward made a century on his debut for Oxfordshire in 2015, when only 15 years old. He joined the Sussex Academy and went on to sign for Sussex, where he has impressed in white ball cricket.

Zach Lion-Cachet is another who played youth cricket at Abingdon Vale and progressed into the Sussex Academy. Zach came to the fore in 2023 when he scored centuries for Oxfordshire in all three formats, before batting well in his first game for Sussex in the Metro Bank One-Day Cup against Worcestershire.

The stories of these cricketers will be told in the future. Looking back, it can be seen that Abingdon Vale gave them a helping hand, providing them with a good grounding in youth cricket and an early chance for both sets of brothers to play in the adult game. As the Oxfordshire Head Coach Rupert Evans commented, 'Abingdon Vale have good coaches, but it's just amazing that one cricket club has produced all these lads.' It would be a mistake to over-emphasise Abingdon Vale's influence, but with its high-quality youth section, it has acted as a successful feeder club, sending off some of its young players to bigger things.

Many of the lads who started out at Abingdon Vale did not forget their Oxfordshire roots when their home county reached the final of the National Counties Twenty20 competition in 2022. Harrison Ward, Luke Charlesworth, Tom Price and Ollie Price, together with the young Sussex player James Coles, all secured release from their first-class clubs in order to play in this final against Cambridgeshire. With left-arm spinner Coles taking three cheap wickets, Cambridgeshire posted a total of 169 for nine, but a well struck 84 from Harrison Ward helped Oxfordshire home, to win in the last over. As their careers progress, these young players will surely go on to further success, although probably not again in an Oxfordshire shirt.

Oxfordshire NCCA Twenty20 winners, 2022.
L-R Paul Whie (Assistant coach), Harrison Ward, Luke Charlesworth,
Ollie Price, Tom Price.

Harrison Ward b 1999

Ben Charlesworth b 2000

Tom Price b 2000

Ollie Price b 2001

Luke Charlesworth b 2003

Zach Lion-Cachet b 2003

The Well-Schooled New Generation

In the 1820s, some of the poorly educated working men of Cowley began to earn money as practice bowlers for the well-to-do Oxford University student cricketers. As their skills developed and the game of cricket grew, opportunities arose for Oxford's best cricketers to play professionally, both locally and around the country.

Come the 1920s, Oxford was producing a string of fine professional first-class county cricketers. These players continued to be largely from working-class backgrounds, or perhaps a notch up, and had only received a basic education at their local schools.

By the 2020s, Oxford has a very different cricketing landscape. The talented young professional cricketers that have emerged over the last few years have all been well-educated, having come through private schools in the city. Harrison Ward, Miles Hammond, Ben and Luke Charlesworth all attended St Edward's School. Tom and Ollie Price went to Magdalen College School, as did Sussex's Aylesbury-born allrounder James Coles. Seam bowler Tom Scriven is another Oxford-born, former Magdalen College schoolboy who has become a professional cricketer, making his first-class debut for Hampshire in 2020 before moving to Leicestershire.

The private schools in and around Oxford have been producing first-class cricketers for a long time. Radley College, to the south of the city, has current first-class cricketers amongst its alumni and going back a generation Middlesex had three former Radley schoolboys in its side.

The combination of great practice and playing facilities, with high quality coaching, has meant that private schools can provide a top-class cricketing education. These days the standard of the facilities is the best that it has ever been and some private schools can be seen as cricket academies.

Historically, a large number of English first-class cricketers have come through the private schools. Up until the amateur status in English cricket was abolished in 1962, nearly all of the first-class cricketers who had come from private schools played as amateurs. Thus, private schools have always been a breeding ground for a large number of cricketers: it is just that nowadays they play as professionals rather than amateurs. What is noteworthy in the Oxford area, however, is that it has been almost exclusively private schoolboys that have broken through into the professional game in recent times.

Whilst the private schools have done a great job, the 93% of the population that has not been privately educated seems to be missing out. Little or no organised cricket is played at state secondary schools and so it is dependent on local clubs to provide youth cricket, but in the city of Oxford those clubs are few and far between. The development of the old Cowley cricketers, from David Burrin through to Neville Rogers, was supported by the strong local cricketing heritage in Cowley and its plentiful clubs and grounds. These days a child growing up in the now multi-cultural district of Cowley has far fewer opportunities to play cricket. At the bottom level, Oxfordshire Cricket has run Street Cricket sessions in Cowley and Blackbird Leys, and there are also soft ball schemes to enable young children to start playing the game. Despite these efforts, there is clearly still a big job to do in Oxford, in spreading the game to include children of all backgrounds and schooling, before identifying young cricketers of potential and progressing them into the county coaching system and age group teams ... which perhaps could lead on to a professional career.

First-class professionals born in Oxford

Name	Seasons played 1st class	Teams
William Burrin	1843	Oxford University
Charles Rogers	1858	Manchester
William Perry	1865	Lancashire
Levi Wight	1883-1909	Derbyshire
William Smith	1900-1914	Surrey
Harry Huggins	1901-1921	Gloucestershire
Alec Bowell	1902-1927	Hampshire
George Brown	1908-1933	Hampshire and England
Jack Parsons	1910-1936	Warwickshire
Edwin Wakelin	1910	Worcestershire
Tom Shepherd	1919-1932	Surrey
Norman Bowell	1924-1925	Hampshire and Northamptonshire
Johnny Arnold	1929-1950	Hampshire and England
Joseph Rogers	1929-1933	Gloucestershire
Neville Rogers	1946-1955	Hampshire
Alan Castell	1961-1971	Hampshire
John Martin	1962-1965	Oxford University and Somerset
David Ligertwood	1992-1996	Surrey and Durham
Robert Cunliffe	1994-2003	Gloucestershire and Leicestershire
Simon Cook	1999-2012	Middlesex and Kent
Ben Gannon	1999-2003	Gloucestershire and Middlesex
Jack Brooks	2009-2023	Northhamptonshire, Yorkshire, Somerset, Sussex, Worcestershire
Edmund Eckersley	2011-2022	Leicestershire and Durham
George Munsey	2015-	Northamptonshire and Scotland
Ben Charlesworth	2018-	Gloucestershire
Tom Scriven	2020-	Hampshire and Leicestershire
Tom Price	2020-	Gloucestershire
Harrison Ward	2021-	Sussex
Oliver Price	2021-	Gloucestershire
Luke Charlesworth	2023-	Gloucestershire

Oxford born **Charlie Walters**, **David Laitt** and **Mike Nurton** all played first-class cricket, but not as professionals. **Zach Lion-Cachet** has played List A cricket for Sussex.

NB: The Oxford city boundary is taken as it currently exists.

Professionals born in villages just outside Oxford

John Godfrey, born in Garsington.
Oswald Herman, born in Horspath.
Bill Haynes, born in Cuddesdon.
Peter Roebuck, born in Oddington.

Please note that these lists might not be comprehensive!

Acknowledgements

Thanks to: Bob Herman and Roger Laitt for sharing memories of their fathers. Dave Strong for stories of his grandfather George Brown and Julie Facey for her research on the Brown family. Rupert Evans, Alan Castell, Mike Nurton, Dave Ligertwood, the late Terry Strange, and the late Alan Rayment, for recollections about their cricket careers. Dr Tim King for providing extensive archive material about his large family. Paul White of Abingdon Vale CC, Roger Mitty of Cumnor CC, Tom Smith of Vincent's Club, Robert Curphey at the MCC Library, and Lindsay McCormack, Archivist at Magdalen College School, who have all been a great help. Julian Lawton-Smith for his support, Jeremy Lonsdale for his work in getting this book into print and Christine for her technical skills and patience.

Some photographs have been taken by the author and others are from his collection. There are also some from the collection of the late Roger Mann. Thanks to Jeremy Lonsdale and Nick Pinhol for permission to use their photographs and also to Dr Tim King, Alan Castell and Bob Herman for providing some of their personal photographs. The image on the cover of Merton College, Oxford is courtesy of iStock.

Bibliography

Books

A History of the County of Oxford: Volume 4, the City of Oxford, Victoria County History, London, 1979

Altham HS, Arlott J, Eagar EDR, Webber R, Hampshire County Cricket, The Sportsman's Book Club, 1958

Arlott, J, John Arlott's Book of Cricketers, Sphere Books Ltd, 1979

Barty-King, Hugh, Quilt Winders and Pod Shavers: History of Cricket Ball and Bat Making, The Book Service Ltd, 1979

Bolton, Geoffrey, History of the OUCC, Holywell Press, 1962

Cowley St John Centenary Handbook 1987

Howat, Gerald, Cricketer Militant: The Life of Jack Parsons, North Moreton Press, 1980

Lawton Smith, Julian, Oxfordshire County Cricket Club – 100 Years of Minor Counties Cricket

Mandle, W, The Professional Cricketer in England in the Nineteenth Century, Liverpool University Press, 1972

Mordaunt Crook, J, Brasenose the Biography of an Oxford College, Oxford University Press, 2008

Nurton, Mike, Conjuring Runs, 1999

Pawle, Gerald, RES Wyatt, Fighting Cricketer. George Allen & Unwin, 1985

Pineo, Richard, North Oxford CC History 1900 – 1995

Pycroft, Rev James, Oxford Memories, Richard Bentley & Son, 1886

Ranjitsinhji, K, The Jubilee Book of Cricket, William Blackwood & Sons, 1907

Rendell, Brian, Fuller Pilch: A Straightforward Man, ACS Publications, 2010

Richards, Graham, 50 Years at Oxford, AuthorHouse, 2011

Richards, Peter, From Magdalen to Merger, Church in the Market Place Publications, 2004

Salway, Paul, A Novel Match at Cricket: A History of Women's Cricket in an English Shire, 2018

Stanier, R, Magdalen School, Basil Blackwell, 1958

Tiddington Cricket Club 1886 -1986 Centenary Handbook

Williams, Charles, Gentlemen & Players The Death of Amateurism in Cricket, Weidenfeld & Nicholson, 2012

Wisden Cricketers Almanack

Wynne-Thomas, Peter, The History of Hampshire CCC, Christopher Helm, 1988

Online resources

Oxfordshire.cricket

Lizandarcy.co.uk – Bat and Ball makers

Peakfans Blog – Derbyshire Cricket 28/5/20

Citizendium – Cricket events from 1601 to 1700

The Local Answer – Roger Jackson, 24/1/2018

WorldPress.com – Cowley Marsh – Life in the Floodplain
Cambridgecrickethistory.co.uk
ESPNCricinfo
CricketArchive

Podcast
Giving The Game Away podcast – Cam Scott & Joel Barber, 20/12/2020

Newspapers
Oxford Times, Oxford Mail, Jackson's Oxford Journal, Oxfordshire Chronicle & Berks & Bucks Gazette, Oxford Chronicle, Oxford Chronicle & Reading Gazette, Oxford University Herald, Sporting Life & Sportsman, Yorkshire Evening Post, Yorkshire Post

Magazines
The Cricketer, Athletic News, Cricket A Weekly Record of the Game, Beyond The Boundaries – PCA

Archives
Oxford University CC/Magdalen Cricket Club, Oxfordshire History Centre
Hampshire CCC Archive, Hampshire Records Office, Winchester
Brasenose College, Oxford
Christ Church, Oxford

Theses/Reports
Sherman, Matt, *The Evolution of Cricket in Oxford,* Kellogg College, Oxford, 2007

Threlfall-Sykes, Judy, *A History of English Women's Cricket, 1880-1939,* De Montfort University, 2015

Independent Commission for Equity in Cricket – *Holding Up a Mirror to Cricket,* June 2023

Cricket Scheme for Oxford Elementary Schools – 10th Annual Report 1930

Index